GUID  S

RT 1
2023

Edited by **Rachel Tranter** and **Olivia Warburton**

15 The Chambers, Vineyard
Abingdon OX14 3FE
brf.org.uk

Bible Reading Fellowship is a charity (233280)
and company limited by guarantee (301324),
registered in England and Wales

ISBN 978 1 80039 1 659

This edition © Bible Reading Fellowship 2022
Cover image © Yotsuya/stock.adobe.com

Distributed in Australia by:
MediaCom Education Inc, PO Box 610, Unley, SA 5061
Tel: 1 800 811 311 | admin@mediacom.org.au

Distributed in New Zealand by:
Scripture Union Wholesale, PO Box 760, Wellington
Tel: 04 385 0421 | suwholesale@clear.net.nz

Acknowledgements

Scripture quotations marked with the following acronyms are taken from the version shown. Where no acronym is given, the quotation is taken from the version stated in the contributor's introduction. NASB: The New American Standard Bible®, copyright © 1960, 1962, 1963, 1968, 1971, 1972, 1973, 1975, 1977, 1995 by The Lockman Foundation. Used by permission. (www.Lockman.org). NRSV: The New Revised Standard Version of the Bible, Anglicised edition, copyright © 1989, 1995 by the Division of Christian Education of the National Council of the Churches of Christ in the United States of America. Used by permission. All rights reserved. ESV: The Holy Bible, English Standard Version, published by HarperCollins Publishers, © 2001 Crossway Bibles, a division of Good News Publishers. Used by permission. All rights reserved. RNJB: The Revised New Jerusalem Bible © 2018, 2019 by Darton, Longman & Todd Ltd. NIV: The Holy Bible, New International Version (Anglicised edition) copyright © 1979, 1984, 2011 by Biblica. Used by permission of Hodder & Stoughton Publishers, a Hachette UK company. All rights reserved. 'NIV' is a registered trademark of Biblica. UK trademark number 1448790.

Every effort has been made to trace and contact copyright owners for material used in this resource. We apologise for any inadvertent omissions or errors, and would ask those concerned to contact us so that full acknowledgement can be made in the future.

A catalogue record for this book is available from the British Library

Printed by Gutenberg Press, Tarxien, Malta

Suggestions for using *Guidelines*

Set aside a regular time and place, if possible, when and where you can read and pray undisturbed. Before you begin, take time to be still and, if you find it helpful, use the BRF prayer on page 6.

In *Guidelines*, the introductory section provides context for the passages or themes to be studied, while the units of comment can be used daily, weekly or whatever best fits your timetable. You will need a Bible (more than one if you want to compare different translations) as Bible passages are not included. Please don't be tempted to skip the Bible reading because you know the passage well. We will have utterly failed if we don't bring our readers into engagement with the word of God. At the end of each week is a 'Guidelines' section, offering further thoughts about or practical application of what you have been studying.

Occasionally, you may read something in *Guidelines* that you find particularly challenging, even uncomfortable. This is inevitable in a series of notes which draws on a wide spectrum of contributors and doesn't believe in ducking difficult issues. Indeed, we believe that *Guidelines* readers much prefer thought-provoking material to a bland diet that only confirms what they already think.

If you do disagree with a contributor, you may find it helpful to go through these three steps. First, think about why you feel uncomfortable. Perhaps this is an idea that is new to you, or you are not happy about the way something has been expressed. Or there may be something more substantial – you may feel that the writer is guilty of sweeping generalisation, factual error, or theological or ethical misjudgement. Second, pray that God would use this disagreement to teach you more about his word and about yourself. Third, have a deeper read about the issue. There are further reading suggestions at the end of each writer's block of notes. And then, do feel free to write to the contributor or the editor of *Guidelines*. We welcome communication, by email, phone or letter, as it enables us to discover what has been useful, challenging or infuriating for our readers. We don't always promise to change things, but we will always listen and think about your ideas, complaints or suggestions. Thank you!

To send feedback, please email **enquiries@brf.org.uk**, phone **+44 (0)1865 319700** or write to the address shown opposite.

Writers in this issue

Valerie Hobbs is a linguist at the University of Sheffield and author of *An Introduction to Religious Language* (Bloomsbury, 2021). Her next book is about gender-based violence within Christian white male supremacy. In her spare time, she enjoys writing about the Bible at **lampofthelamb.com**.

Andy Angel is the vicar of St Andrew's, Burgess Hill. Previously, he taught New Testament in two Anglican training colleges and has written various books including *Playing with Dragons* (Cascade Books, 2014) and *The Jesus You Really Didn't Know* (Cascade Books, 2019).

Isabelle Hamley is theological adviser to the House of Bishops (Church of England), after being chaplain to the archbishop of Canterbury, a vicar, a theological college lecturer and a university chaplain.

Stephen Finamore is principal of Bristol Baptist College. He is married to Rebecca and has two daughters. Steve has worked as a pastor, a lawyer and in community development in inner London and the Peruvian Andes.

David Spriggs was minister of a Baptist church until his retirement. He continues to enjoy engaging with the Bible as he has done throughout his ministry in local churches and for the Evangelical Alliance and Bible Society.

Philip Grasham is a freelance Bible teacher and writer. He has worked for three different UK theological colleges and was a mission trainer with BMS World Mission. He and his wife also spent twelve years with WEC International including working in West Africa among Muslim nomads.

Pauline Hoggarth was born in Peru, where her parents were missionaries. She taught modern languages in Scotland and London and worked with Scripture Union in the UK and overseas for 23 years. She is the author of *The Seed and the Soil* (Langham, 2011).

Tim Judson is a Baptist minister based at Honiton Family Church in east Devon.

Henry Wansbrough is a monk of Ampleforth, Yorkshire. He has been chairman of the Oxford Faculty of Theology and has also served on the Pope's Biblical Commission and on the Anglican Roman Catholic International Commission.

Richard Martin served with the Church Army before ordination to a curacy and an incumbency in Gravesend. He is now priest-in-charge of three parishes in the Gloucester Diocese and is a Third Order Franciscan.

Johannes J. Knecht (PhD, University of St Andrews) is dean of postgraduate studies at WTC Theology and specialises in church history and systematic theology. His primary interests are patristics, Christology and trinitarian theology.

The editors write...

As the world becomes an ever more complicated place to live, it is so important that we remember why we are studying the Bible and God's word to us. Jesus reminds us that, ultimately, it is about love – for our neighbours and for ourselves. In our globalised society, can we say that there is anyone who isn't our 'neighbour'?

Philip Grasham helps us to think about this with his notes in this issue on 'traversing time and crossing cultures', helping us to see how our interpretations have been shaped by the culture around us. Valerie Hobbs also offers notes on 'training our eyes for heaven', helping us to focus on the long story of God's salvation plan without losing our focus on what matters in this life.

This issue offers some further important themes to ponder on the approach to Easter. Tim Judson explains why 'Christian' lament is so important and how we can engage with this often-overlooked aspect of our faith. Meanwhile, Henry Wansbrough looks at repentance and forgiveness, with a particular focus on acts of generosity and extending forgiveness to others.

Other notes in this issue take us deep into the Old Testament. We first continue Isabelle Hamley's excellent series of Judges. She has titled her notes 'justice and mercy in the promised land', and we indeed find these as she walks us through this difficult book. Pauline Hoggarth dedicates two weeks to four of the minor prophets: Jonah, Haggai, Nahum and Habakkuk. These four very different prophets can all teach us something about our world today.

We spend most of this issue in the New Testament. Andy Angel starts a new gospel series on Matthew, beginning with chapters 15—18. In great detail, he takes us through the Pharisees' questioning of Jesus, Jesus' teaching to his disciples and other gems along the way. Stephen Finamore continues his engaging series on Romans and new writer Johannes J. Knecht looks at the letter to the Colossians. In the previous issue David Spriggs explored twin parables, and now he looks at 'internal twin parables' – twins that appear within one parable.

Finally, Richard Martin offers us a week post-Easter to celebrate and reflect on the resurrection. As we ponder this great mystery of our faith, our prayer is that you would be empowered to take the love of God, the love that he displayed through Jesus, to your neighbours and to the world.

The BRF Prayer

Faithful God,
thank you for growing BRF
from small beginnings
into a worldwide family of ministries.
We rejoice as young and old
discover you through your word
and grow daily in faith and love.
Keep us humble in your service,
ambitious for your glory
and open to new opportunities.
For your name's sake,
Amen

Training our eyes for heaven

Valerie Hobbs

'How can you miss what you've never had?'

In 'Tiny Love Stories' in *The New York Times*, a recently divorced woman reflects on this question from her therapist, as she grieves over the shared meals she and her husband rarely had during their marriage. The therapist probes further: 'Is that what you missed as a child?' Yes, she replies, finally letting herself mourn her past and present.

This is a human mystery: missing what we've never had.

God distributes his love generously and with purpose. Immediately after Adam and Eve fell, God clothed and fed his broken children, guiding their hands through the first sad sacrifice of animals, a sign of the redemption they now needed. As God's story of rescue continued, he offered yet more such signs: an ark for safe passage through watery judgement; freedom from Egyptian slavery; manna from heaven; water from a rock; deliverance from exile; Jesus' healing hands. Great is his faithfulness. God gives and gives, his memory of his promises never failing, his every physical provision training the tear-stained eyes, worn hands, hungry stomachs and broken hearts of his people towards their future: complete restoration in body and soul.

By grace, through faith in Jesus Christ, the gift of salvation opens our eyes to the wonders of our eternal home with God. And in this world of suffering, we long for that day when all will be well. While we wait in this wounded world, we are Christ's hands and feet. This series reflects on this space of tension, fixed anxiously between earth and heaven, where God in his kindness communicates through our actions of peace, love and compassion for our neighbour. He stirs up a longing for things they too have never had, and through us trains their eyes for heaven.

Unless otherwise stated, Bible quotations are taken from the NASB.

1 The weight of waiting

1 Kings 8:33–36

January is not usually the time we Christians think about waiting. The four Sundays before Christmas are set aside for this, together with Lent, and are periods when we anticipate Christ's birth and his death and resurrection respectively. But at times the Spirit disrupts our rhythmic remembering, unsettles and unseats us in glorious unpredictability.

Solomon's prophetic prayer of dedication in 1 Kings 8 presents one such opportunity. I was prompted to read it again, having waded to the end of 2 Kings, where the tribe of Judah is led into Babylonian captivity. Though God does not leave us without hope at the end of this period of redemptive history, it's difficult reading. The epic books of Kings are full of idolatry, violence, cruelty and corruption.

All this attests powerfully to our need for a saviour. But after Babylon captured them, God's people would have to wait 70 years before they could return to their land and rebuild the temple. And even then, the Messiah did not appear. By the time the angel appeared to Mary, mother of God, the people had waited for 400 years. As in the time of Samuel, 'word from the Lord was rare in those days; visions were infrequent' (1 Samuel 3:1). Many lost hope.

For we who live in the new covenant, there has never been a better time for waiting. In Christ we have seen heaven reach down and angels descend. Our Saviour is on the scene, his word completed, our salvation secured, his promises renewed. Jesus has begun his spiritual reign on the earth, and we have the full, written revelation of God. 'You are already filled, you have already become rich, you have become kings without us' (1 Corinthians 4:8)!

And yet this world is still in the way. 'The Lord has said that he would dwell in the thick darkness' (1 Kings 8:12), but at times the heavens seem shut and there is no rain (1 Kings 8:35). On these days we feel the weight of waiting. We wrestle with God. We will not let him go until he blesses us.

2 God's kingdom has come near

Luke 10:1–16; Exodus 3:1–9

The phrase 'come near' in Luke 10:9 and 11 is common throughout the Bible. One well-known early instance is in Exodus 3, when God calls to Moses from the burning bush, warning, 'Do not come near here.' Moses must remove his sandals, discarding the dust of the earth his feet had carried to see this marvellous sight (v. 5), giving himself up entirely in reverence and respect to holy ground. Later, Moses alone is permitted to come near to the Lord, while 70 of Israel's elders worship at a distance (Exodus 24:1–2).

In this phrase 'come near,' then, the Bible holds in tension these two: holiness and intimacy. In the former is a sacred presence near to which no evil nor plague can come (Psalm 91:9–11), a God whose day draws near and comes as destruction (Joel 1:15). And yet in the latter is this same God, a loving Father who comes near to we who welcomed evil into humankind's first sacred dwelling place.

Jesus's words then, to 70 kingdom labourers, come ripe with all this meaning. Whatever city they enter, they are to say, 'The kingdom of God has come near to you.' Following Moses, these kingdom-bearers were likewise instructed to remove their shoes (Luke 10:4) and all other worldly dependence, giving themselves up entirely to the hospitality of any person of peace. In the dwelling places of such people, the 70 are to heal the sick, a reminder that in God our refuge, no plague will come near (Luke 10:9). This is no prosperity gospel, but rather pure and undefiled religion, works of love that flow out of the gift of faith. As God's people regift this spiritual and material refreshment, we share a glimpse of the kingdom come near, the kingdom to come.

Yet for those who do not receive Christ's labourers in peace, 'who say, "Keep to yourself, do not come near me, For I am holier than you!"' (Isaiah 65:5a), the kingdom coming near brings only judgement. Such people are smoke in God's nostrils, 'a fire that burns all the day' (Isaiah 65:5b). The dust of their cities God's labourers must wipe off in protest and leave behind, as Moses did (Luke 10:11). We do not rejoice in this, only that our names are recorded in heaven. For this promise we labour, for the present life and for the life to come, fixing our hope on the living God.

3 The only good Samaritan

Luke 10:25–37

An expert in Mosaic law tries to test Jesus, wanting to justify himself. He knows the law and articulates it in perfect orthodoxy, yet cannot grasp that deeper truth which only the Spirit can inscribe on any human heart. Speaking in parable, Jesus' multilayered answer turns this lawyer's question on its head. 'Who is my neighbour?' becomes 'Who proved to be a neighbour?'

Above all, the parable presents the gospel, Jesus' story of himself, a man travelling from Jerusalem, city of God, to Jericho, city of Canaan. The road Jesus references was well-known to all Jews, bordering the tribes of Judah and Benjamin, a thoroughfare for pilgrims travelling up to Jerusalem for holy days. Yet we must not miss the imagery here. This man is 'going down' (v. 30), tracing the fall of Adam, and the fate that follows leaves him lower still. He falls among robbers, who strip and beat him, leaving him half-dead. The wounded man's next human encounters mirror the trajectory of his journey. First his own people, a priest and a Levite, by chance come upon him yet do not receive him. They hide their faces, passing him by.

A Samaritan is next to discover the man, yet, seeing his wounded body, is stirred with compassion. Here the next layer of the parable begins to crystallise as Jesus, wounded, despised, rejected, likewise takes up his post as ultimate outsider, the Samaritan Saviour. His healing hands bandage the man's wounds, lift him to his own beast and pass him into the safekeeping of a carer, with a promise to return.

Who proved to be a neighbour? Not the religious establishment, who abandoned and despised the Holy One of Israel. No, only Jesus is the good neighbour. For our sake he was delivered over to death at the hands of cruel men, now raised to life. Forsaken and dying, we who fell first in Adam find rescue from sin, are established and anointed in Christ (Romans 5:12).

Jesus' final words to the lawyer contain our marching orders: 'Go and do the same.' Show mercy as we have received mercy. To the hungry we bring food, even the bread of life. To the thirsty we carry drink, even rivers of living water. To the stranger we offer an invitation, even to Christ's kingdom. To the naked we give clothing, even our Saviour's kingly robes. Truly, as we do these things for those society despises, we do them for Jesus.

4 As in heaven, also on earth

Matthew 6:1–13

Across seven petitions (perfection) in three parts (completion), Jesus' model prayer draws us close to the edge of something unfathomable and altogether spectacular. Within the prayer is a careful structure, placing each petition next to its counterpart, revealing its meaning. In the first pair, we ask for the honour of God's name and deliverance from the one whose name is evil (v. 9b, 13b). In the second, we pray for God's kingdom to come and deliverance from temptation to stray from his holy presence (v. 10a, 13a). In the third pair, we ask that God's will be done, as in heaven, also on earth (v. 10b). Within the prayer's structure, Jesus positions this petition against one for forgiveness from sin, as we forgive those who sin against us (v. 12a). We see here that the heart of God's will is peace between humankind and the divine.

What is the path to this peace? Jesus has patterned his prayer after the ten commandments, which begin with recognition of who God is and end with how we can honour God through human relationships. But more than the law's letter, Jesus offers us a re-encounter of the law through the eyes of our salvation. We see this in the centre of the Lord's Prayer, with the request for bread. Exodus 16 lays the groundwork. In the wilderness, God gave the Israelites their bread for sabbath rest a day early. And by surpassing their earthly need that day, by calling their minds to a coming rest, God was teaching his people of a need and a rest far greater. This is why when Jesus came, he said, 'I am the bread of life; the one who comes to me will not be hungry' (John 6:35). A truer translation of Jesus's words in verse 11 are therefore these: 'Give us tomorrow's bread, today.'

In our own worldly wilderness, God gives us too a taste of future promise through the gift of Jesus today. In Jesus is the summing up of all things, things in heaven and things on earth (Ephesians 1:10). Indeed, Jesus incarnate is heaven on earth, God's in-dwelling of creation in human form, an honour he shares, by the Spirit, with the new temple, his body, the church. These gifts we pass on eagerly, our earthly and heavenly bread, without any showiness. Our hope is that those we meet might taste and see as we do, that God exercises loving-kindness, justice and righteousness as in heaven, also on earth. He delights in these things (Jeremiah 9:23–24).

5 Those who see the sun

Ecclesiastes 1:1–9

Ecclesiastes is medicine for the wounded and their helpers and especially for those with visions of empire. Grand designs! High hopes! Victorious visions! We set out to overturn oppressors, rescue castaways, sort out all the systems, win the world! Ecclesiastes speaks back. 'Vanity of vanities,' its writer declares. 'All is futility [or "vanity"]' (1:2). 'The sun rises and the sun sets… on its circular courses the wind returns… to the place where the rivers flow, there they flow again… So there is nothing new under the sun' (1:5–9).

'Under the sun' – this phrase pervades this enigmatic book. Indeed, Ecclesiastes refers to the 'sun' more than any other book of the Bible. Its constant companion is the theme of human labour. 'What advantage does a person have in all his work which he does under the sun?' asks this son of David (1:3). His words evoke David's own meditations on the symbolism of the sun. God himself is depicted as the sun (Psalm 84:11), its heat scorching the people of the earth, who respond by blaspheming God (Revelation 16:9). 'There is nothing hidden from its heat' (Psalm 19:6; compare Jonah 4:8).

All this the writer of Ecclesiastes meditates on, laments over. He's seen all the oppressive acts under the sun, all the tears they trigger. In the place of justice and righteousness is wickedness. Even through intense labour, no human can discover the full meaning of all this, even the wisest man (8:17). Rest is elusive and brings only poverty. Only death seems certain, ushering the cancellation of all our toil under the sun (2:18–36), all earth's fruit sprung from rivalry between each human and their neighbour (4:4). Ecclesiastes isn't going to gaslight you, dear reader. All is vanity. The living take this to heart (7:2).

Yet here is the tension: that by the tender mercy of our God, there is another light, the sun of righteousness, the sunrise from on high, the lamp of the Lamb. Under this Son, neither our preaching nor our faith is vanity (1 Corinthians 15:14), though even in kingdom work, God alone knows when we labour on stones and when on good soil. Many times we cannot tell the difference. Still, Jesus says that when our effort meets adversity, the peace we've offered returns to us (Luke 10:6). What mystery! The wisdom of Christ, our imperishable inheritance – these are good and an advantage to those who see the sun (Ecclesiastes 7:11).

6 I will be found by you

One sum of heaven's story is this: finding what is lost. Lost paradise, lost coin, lost sheep, lost rest, lost joy, lost hope.

Banished from God's garden, enslaved to sin and death, God's people were scattered from one end of the earth to the other. In exile, we find no repose, only an anxious mind, eyes weary with longing, a despairing heart. Night after night, we dissolve our couch with tears (Psalm 6:6). We seek him whom our soul loves. We call for him, but he does not answer. 'We are passing away, we are perishing, we are all perishing!' (Numbers 17:12)

Yet this is no purely linear plot. Rather, the Bible tells and retells God's story of lost and found, the same hope to every generation, one people found and bound together by one perfect set of promises. Jeremiah 29 communicates this clearly. Here is the prophet's letter, written from Jerusalem, city of God, portrait of the heavenly realm, addressed to those in exile, all who survive. Here is God's letter to us, and here are his instructions:

Build houses and settle down. Plant gardens and eat their produce. Marry and multiply. Seek the peace and prosperity of this earthly city. As it prospers, we prosper. And finally, a warning. Watch out for those who tell lies in God's name. 'I have not sent them,' declares the Lord.

JEREMIAH 29:5–9 (paraphrased)

And here is God's oath fulfilled, a glimpse of heaven and earth made new:

I will be found by you and will bring you back from captivity. I will gather you from all the nations and places where I have banished you and will bring you back to the place from which I carried you into exile.

JEREMIAH 29:11–14 (paraphrased)

We will find refuge. We will find our joy in the Lord. Seek and we will find. Ask for the ancient paths. Ask where the good way is. Walk in it, and you will find rest for your souls (Jeremiah 6:16). Yes, we will find rest.

What is this way? How will God be found by us? 'The first thing Andrew did was to find his brother Simon and tell him, "We have found the Messiah"… He brought him to Jesus' (John 1:41–42, NIV). Layer upon layer, story after story, this is God's masterpiece of lost and found. Having found our Saviour, we have become in his eyes as one who finds peace.

Guidelines

This week's set of notes have probed that unsettling space between the whole earth's groans for glory, the Spirit's current in-dwelling among God's people and the hope of Jesus' return. To walk alongside someone in love, to train their eyes for heaven, so often involves sitting with them in that place of unrest, holding grief and joy together, informing each other. This is no easy task, especially in a society that presses us to rush past pain and loss, quick fix, chin up, stiff upper lip, keep calm and carry on.

- What sadness are you suppressing? What hurt do those around you carry quietly?
- Have you had any offers of peace rejected?
- What glimpses of heaven have you encountered recently?
- Reflect on the sorrow and joy around you, considering them in light of Jesus' own words about this space of tension in Matthew 5:3–6.

Matthew 15—18

Andy Angel

In the second half of his gospel, Matthew continues to develop his overarching theme of Jesus as the true teacher. Our opening story has him in conflict with the Pharisees over exactly how we ought to live out obedience to God's commandments (Matthew 15:1–20). He warns his disciples against the teaching of the Pharisees and Sadducees (Matthew 16:5–12). He teaches his disciples how to live together as the church community that he will build on Peter the rock (Matthew 18; compare Matthew 16:18), in the fourth of the five blocks into which Matthew puts most of Jesus' teaching.

Jesus also reveals to his disciples more of his identity. Through his general ministry (Matthew 15:29–31) and the feeding of the four thousand (Matthew 15:32–39 and 16:5–12) he continues to act in ways that reveal who he truly is. He brings this to a head with his disciples in the question he asks them at Caesarea Philippi (Matthew 16:13–20): 'Who do you say that I am?' God the Father reveals to the inner circle of Jesus' disciples (Peter, James and John) that Jesus is his Son and that, as Son of God and true teacher of the law, they are to listen to him (Matthew 17:1–8).

As Jesus reveals more of his own identity, he begins to unpack to the disciples some aspects of their own identity as disciples that they have not really understood up until this point – and which they find profoundly challenging and disturbing. Jesus tells his disciples that as the Messiah, he will not fit the contemporary expectations of a victorious king or ruler-priest, which were the dominant messianic expectations of the time. Rather, he would be arrested, tortured and killed before rising again on the third day (Matthew 16:21, 17:9 and 17:22–23). He begins to explain to his disciples that their vocation is also to carry their crosses (Matthew 16:24–26). He develops the theme of the community of disciples who voluntarily lay down any power they possess to build a community of grace. The vision is gritty and challenging but ultimately a practical vision which embodies mercy and love in our relationships with one another as disciples of Christ.

Unless otherwise stated, Bible quotations are taken from the NRSV.

1 Seeing Pharisaism in the mirror

Matthew 15:1–20

The Pharisees get a bad rap in too many Christian circles. We still get them wrong and get Jesus' critique of them wrong. Much as it may stick in our throats, Jesus occasionally paid the Pharisees compliments – even for their teaching (Matthew 23:2–3a). Jesus taught commandments from the Torah, just like the Pharisees (e.g., Matthew 5:21–26). Jesus obeyed the law, just like the Pharisees sought to (note that Jesus had fringes on his garment [Matthew 14:36], as Deuteronomy 22:12 commanded). So, when we approach today's text, we need to ensure that we read it for what it actually says.

The key to understanding this text lies in verse 20, where Jesus says, 'These are what defile a person, but to eat with unwashed hands does not defile.' We too easily fall into the trap of assuming that the Pharisees are presenting Jesus with 'the law' and that Jesus teaches 'love' instead of 'the law'. But actually, the Pharisees here present Jesus with their own addition to the law. The law never says people have to eat their daily food with washed hands. And Jesus does not critique the Pharisees for obeying the law. He criticises them for not obeying the law and replacing the commandments of the law with their own additions to the law (verses 3–6). So, Jesus actually teaches that we should keep God's commandments and avoid replacing them with our own ideas.

What the Pharisees were doing seems really quite sensible. They were creating a hedge around the law – a set of extra commands to help you obey God's commandments and avoid disobeying them. At least, it seems sensible enough in practice to many Christians that we do exactly the same thing. If you don't believe me, browse the shelves of a Christian bookshop. You will find many additions to Jesus' teaching on prayer. You will find many books adding to Jesus' teaching on relationships. So, let's make sure we are humble as we read what Jesus has to say to the Pharisees here, learn from their mistakes, and listen to Jesus' words more than anyone else's.

2 Focus

Sometimes Jesus' behaviour is puzzling – even after it is explained. Some of us might be shocked that Jesus refuses to respond to this woman. We might accuse Jesus of being racist or sexist here. A foreign woman desperately needs his help and he does not even answer her cries. Some might applaud the woman for persisting. We could be tempted to make her the heroine of this story. Perhaps claim that faith looks like this – after all, she kneels before him to make her request when she gets his attention. We might speculate that the brilliance of her reply earns her the healing for her daughter she so desperately seeks. Maybe even suggest that faith entails getting the attention of a God who does not always seem to listen – to demand from God by any means.

But to draw these kind of conclusions misses what was going on. Jesus was focused. 'I was sent only to the lost sheep of the house of Israel' (v. 24). He could not be clearer. God has sent him to minister to the people of Israel who are currently lost in their sin and consequently under divine judgement. He calls them back to faith. Jesus perceives this mission as urgent (see Matthew 10:23; 16:28; 24:34) and wants to obey his heavenly Father without getting distracted. In the moment, however, he is distracted. Seeing faith outside the people of God once again (compare Matthew 8:5–13), he heals the woman's daughter.

The story can feel slightly uncomfortable, but perhaps there is wisdom in it we might need to recognise. How many ministers receive criticism from their congregations for trying to do too many things (and not enough of the things which those criticising want them to do)? How many ministers lose the focus God has given them under the weight of the criticisms of church members (who often do not agree among themselves)? Focusing on some things means not attending to others. God has a plan for the Gentiles, as we discover later in Matthew. Perhaps more of us ought to focus for the moment on what God wants. Perhaps more of us ought to trust our ministers to do the same.

3 Seeing and believing

Scattered throughout the gospels, there are summary verses which give a snapshot of Jesus' ministry or which summarise an event in just a few words without seeming to tell the story. It is easy to pass over these as if they have little to say, but that would be a mistake. Often, they contain hidden gems which we only see if we are deeply immersed in the Bible (or have a good commentary to hand). This is one such summary passage.

Jesus sits down. Whether he intends to rest or to teach the crowds that will come to him, we do not know; Matthew does not tell us. What we do know is that the crowds bring many sick people to Jesus, and that he heals them. Although the crowd brought these people to Jesus in the hope that he would heal them, they are amazed when they see the mute speaking, the maimed made whole, the lame wandering around and the blind seeing things (v. 31). Matthew recalls the Greek version of Isaiah 35:5–6 here as those verses prophesy the same kinds of healing miracles using three of the same (Greek) terms: mute (*kōphos*), lame (*chōlos*) and blind (*tuphlos*). In making this connection, Matthew pictures Jesus as doing the things which will happen at the time when God restores his people, taking them out of exile in Babylon and bringing them back to Zion – the land of promise, of milk and honey.

It is just a hint, and much as many in Israel were hoping for a different outcome from Jesus' ministry (political liberation rather than crucifixion, for example), it is a signal that there is more to Jesus than meets the eye. The crowds praise the God of Israel as their friends and relatives are healed. This action (much as it is wonderful) shows that they did not realise that, in Jesus, God himself was among them. Jesus does not blame them, as this is part of the work that he has come to do. Instead, he seeks to feed them. But as the story progresses, we see the tragic side of this lack of vision. Perhaps we need to ask ourselves what more there is to Jesus than meets our eyes, and what more he might like to teach us.

4 Jesus' compassion

Matthew 15:32–39

There are many puzzles about this story. It is so close to the feeding of the five thousand (Matthew 14:13–21) that some of the wording is identical. The plotlines of the stories are nearly identical. So why does Matthew include this one too? Some have tried to speculate around numbers, suggesting, for example, that five and twelve are Jewish numbers (five books in the Torah and twelve tribes of Israel) and four and seven are Gentile numbers (four corners of the earth and seven is the number for completeness). But the actual number of the Gentile nations is 70 (or 72) in the Jewish traditions of Jesus, so why doesn't that number appear? And completeness is not specifically Gentile. In reality, it is difficult to prove anything from numbers unless the text gives the reader other clues to suggest that numbers have a particular significance, and Matthew does not do that in this story. So it is better to concentrate on what Matthew does say clearly.

One difference between this and the other feeding miracle are Jesus' words in verse 32: 'I have compassion for the crowd.' Jesus looks at these people who have spent three days with him. This must have been an intense time together, given the healing miracles Jesus was doing. But they are now exhausted. Jesus does not want to send them away hungry for fear they might collapse with exhaustion on the way home. He wants to meet their physical needs.

Sometimes we can get so bound up in the incredible miracle that we read here that we miss the point. Sometimes we can get so involved in seeking 'deeper meanings' to solve the kinds of puzzles outlined above that we miss the plain meaning of the text. The point of the miracle is simply to provide because there was no other way of providing. Resources were limited and simply not enough. But this does not stop Jesus caring for the physical needs of those following him. Perhaps in the wake of the coronavirus pandemic, we could take some time to think about this. We are not currently in need of deeper meanings, but we are in need of physical and mental restoration. Perhaps more of us could ask Jesus for a miracle.

5 Signs of the times

Again, we need to be careful of not falling into the trap of demonising the Pharisees (as we have so often done as Christians) without taking a good hard look at our own behaviour in the light of Jesus' criticism. This time, the Pharisees and Sadducees come to Jesus. They ask for a sign from heaven to confirm Jesus' authority is from God. Jesus criticises them for being able to interpret the weather but not being able to read the signs of the times.

The Pharisees were a holiness movement, adding many teachings to the law in order to prevent people from getting anywhere near breaking it. They hoped that God would look on their holiness and bless them with freedom from Roman oppression and God's kingdom would be established throughout the land. The Sadducees believed that only the law should be obeyed, ignoring the more recent Jewish religious writings with visions of the kingdom and resurrection. Jesus criticises them both, promising them only the sign of Jonah. We know from Matthew 12:38–42 what Jesus means. Just as Jonah was three days in the sea monster (Greek: *kētos*), so would Jesus be in the earth, because he has been killed by some of his fellow Jews. As a result, the Gentile Ninevites would condemn them at the resurrection of the dead when Jesus comes to judge the earth – because the Ninevites listened to Jonah and repented. It seems the sin of the Pharisees and Sadducees is not responding to the mercy of God and not repenting and turning to holy living, as both John the Baptist and Jesus have called them to in the light of the coming judgement. They should have taken a leaf out of the Ninevites' book.

So should we. It can be so easy to half-repent – to say sorry without really examining ourselves – and to justify our behaviour rather than ask Jesus to teach us how to change, and then to criticise Jesus where we disagree with his teachings. Certainly some Pharisees were making this mistake, as they took their own additional teachings so seriously that they stopped obeying some of God's commandments. But before we get ready to cast the first stone, we should examine ourselves before God and listen to what Jesus would have us do.

6 Crossed wires

Matthew 16:5–12

The disciples are hungry. They forgot to bring bread. Jesus talks in metaphors, using yeast to make his point. The disciples continue to talk about bread (verse 7 should read: 'and they carried on discussing among themselves, "We've not brought bread"' – other translations add words that are not there in the Greek). Jesus corrects them, pointing out that he was talking about the ways in which people teach how we follow God and interpret his commands, not about bread. Jesus' point is that the disciples should beware the teaching of the Pharisees and Sadducees, as both those groups within the Judaism of the day (much as they disagreed with each other) did not interpret God's commands properly. By the end of the story, the disciples get his point.

Perhaps, though, verses 9 and 10 need some further explanation. If this was all there was to the story and these verses were taken out, the story might seem to flow better. But actually, they add a crucial point. Don't the disciples remember the feeding miracles? Jesus performed the same miracle of multiplication of food twice. What does that remind you of? Who does that remind you of? Who miraculously provided food in the desert for his hungry people? The answer, of course, is that the Lord God provided food in the wilderness for his hungry people when he rescued them from oppression in Egypt.

Who has the right to interpret the law? Who interprets it correctly? Who best knows the ways of God and who can best teach them? Well, God, of course. And this is Jesus' point to his disciples. They should not follow the teachings of the Pharisees and Sadducees as they seek to interpret the law and teach people the ways of God, because God is already among them, teaching them the true interpretation of the law and the true way to live as God calls us to. It is interesting that Matthew notes that the disciples get this point (v. 12; Mark certainly thinks they did not get it). Perhaps as we read Jesus' teachings, and sometimes are tempted to find some book or scholar who can interpret the tricky ones away, we ought to consider what kind of yeast we are buying into.

Guidelines

Questions of Jesus' authority and identity lie all over this week's texts. Does Jesus interpret the law correctly? The Pharisees question this, noting that Jesus' disciples do not follow the teachings that they have placed carefully around the law to help people to remain holy. The Canaanite woman sees that Jesus has power to heal but is little concerned that his calling is to the lost sheep of the house of Israel. The crowds also recognise that Jesus has power to heal and praise the God of Israel for his ministry (though perhaps Matthew hints that in doing this, they do not recognise that Jesus is the God of Israel, 'Immanuel, God with us'). Even the disciples seem a little shaky in their faith. They recently saw Jesus walk on water and acclaimed him the 'Son of God' (Matthew 14:33). But now they are unsure as to whether Jesus will repeat the kind of multiplication of food miracle that they saw only recently. The Pharisees and Sadducees resisted Jesus' call to repentance and so were not convinced his prophetic ministry was valid. They also thought that they knew how to interpret God's law better. That Matthew fills this section of his gospel with stories raising such questions should come as no surprise given what comes next.

But all this raises the same set of questions for us. Who do we think Jesus is… really? Does our understanding of him actually reflect who he claims to be or what others have told us about him or maybe even the songs we sing? Perhaps our picture of Jesus comes from our own values, which might be a funny mix of all the things we have experienced to date and some of what we read and hear in the media. For example, where do we get our ethics from? Radio 4, the newspapers, popular theology, conversations with our friends, the latest buzz book in do-it-yourself therapy? Do we expect Jesus to bring healing into our lives and those of others? Do we seek this and pray for it in practice? Do we recognise that, as God, Jesus has authority over all things in our lives or do we sometimes 'know better'? The stories in this section of Matthew provide us with plenty of food for thought.

1 Who am I?

Matthew 16:13–30

It is an interesting feature of this story that in recognising who Jesus truly is, Peter finds his own identity and mission in life. Jesus asks his disciples two questions. The first question elicits quite a few answers, which seem positive as they compare Jesus with figures generally regarded favourably. It is clear that there is some discussion over who Jesus is, even among people who are drawn towards him. The second question gets a decisive answer from Peter, who realises that Jesus is the 'Messiah, the Son of the living God' (v. 16). Many knew that the Messiah was to liberate Israel from Roman rule, but perhaps fewer knew that the Messiah would train God's people to live out his law in holiness and justice (a hope manifested, for example, in the Psalms of Solomon, written around 60BC by an unknown Jewish author). Whether or not Peter saw Jesus' divine sonship solely in terms of Davidic kingship (compare Psalm 2) or being divine, Matthew does not make clear here, but he does note that Peter only knows this because God the Father has revealed it to him.

With this breakthrough in understanding, Peter then receives a greater understanding of his own identity. Jesus puns on his name 'Peter' (Greek: *Petros*) and the word for rock (Greek: *petra*): Peter will become the rock on which Jesus builds the community of God that gathers for worship, learning God's commands and fighting God's battles (that is what the Greek word for 'church' [*ecclesia*] means in the Greek version of the Old Testament, the Septuagint). Jesus reassures him that the forces of evil ('the gates of Hades') will not overcome God's gathered community.

Jesus also gives Peter authority. There is a lively scholarly discussion about what kind of authority Jesus gives Peter. The closest parallel to the language of binding and loosing is found in the rabbinic language used of teachers interpreting the Torah (binding people to certain forms of behaviour and loosing them from various restrictions). So, it looks as if Jesus gives Peter the authority to continue his (Jesus') own ministry of teaching the true interpretation of the law, and making clear to people how God commands us all to live. As Peter claims Jesus is (among other things) the one person who will teach God's people, he finds himself called into this ministry and empowered for it.

2 Stark truths

With his newfound authority, Peter oversteps the mark. He misunderstands the nature of the spiritual battle in which he will lead God's people. To be fair to Peter, contemporary Jewish understandings of spiritual warfare identified foreign nations with demons or incompetent angels and God's people with the Lord of the angelic armies who would defeat the spiritual forces governing foreign nations (e.g. the War Scroll). Given that Jesus has just commissioned Peter to be the rock on which God's people will stand against evil spiritual forces, we can understand why Peter attempts to correct Jesus' understanding of the spiritual battle. How on earth could Jesus undergo suffering and be killed?

But Jesus transformed (and transforms) every kingdom ideology or spirituality that sees victory as seizing political power. He takes the starkest of images to make his point. People carried their crosses on the way to crucifixion. Crucifixion was a punishment reserved for the lowest people in society, i.e. slaves and terrorists. Jesus makes clear that following him leads to crucifixion. Just because Jesus' disciples ran away, we must not miss the force of this. Jesus knew he was going to be crucified. Would-be messiahs had been crucified before along with their followers. There was every reason for Jesus' hearers to take this literally. Even for those who would not face such an execution, the invitation remains stark: we must be willing to lose our lives, and cling on to nothing in them, if we are to follow Jesus. For justice will be done by the Son of Man when he comes to judge. It is quite impossible to reconcile these words with any idea of Christian spirituality having anything to do with rebellion against political overlords. Hearing this must have been even more shocking for the disciples whose embedded theology was most likely the exact opposite – full of hope for the revolution against Rome.

But this does not mean we give up on justice. Jesus calls us to live just lives, and so spread justice in society. In doing this, we become the light of the world – but in humility. We ask Jesus to teach us all holiness – but with grace towards those who fail. Jesus' vision is anything but apolitical; it is simply not power-hungry or status-obsessed. It is about love.

3 Whose voice fills your mind?

Matthew 17:1–8

We have all sorts of voices going around our heads and our hearts. As one 1980s singer put it, we are under the influence of somebody all of the time – meaning, we take on board ideas and the lifestyles they suggest from all around us, often subconsciously. It is not just the things we watch and read, but the way others live and talk that affects the way we think and live. Sometimes, we do not even realise how strongly influenced we are by others.

The question of whose voice fills your mind is fundamental to understanding this story of the transfiguration of Jesus. Central to the identity of God's people was their listening to the voice of God. They would gather to hear the law read so that they might learn to live it as a community. God sent prophets to speak his word to his community to bring them back on track when they strayed from living as he commanded. It is no coincidence that in this story Jesus is flanked by Moses (who received the law from God and gave it to God's people) on one side and Elijah the prophet on the other.

Nor is it any coincidence that God adds the words he spoke at Jesus' baptism, 'listen to him'. God commands the disciples to listen to Jesus. In Jesus' day, the rabbis were putting a great deal of energy into updating and making sense of the law for their own times. This was a natural thing to do, as by the time of Jesus, the law (or, at least, elements of it) was a thousand years old – and times changed back then, just as they do today. In this process of interpreting the law, the rabbis grappled with difficult problems, such as exactly how to work out divorce fairly. We have already seen that Jesus cuts through some of this activity with his own final word on how to interpret God's law. We try to update and interpret the Bible in ways not so unlike the rabbis. Into all this activity, God speaks to us as he did to that inner circle of disciples: 'this is my Son, the Beloved… listen to him'.

4 One piece at a time

Matthew 17:9–13

Sometimes the pieces of the puzzle don't all come together at once. They come together piece by piece until the picture begins to emerge and we understand what we are meant to see. This story talks us through another piece of the puzzle coming into place for the disciples. Jesus commands them not to mention the vision to anyone until after his resurrection. The disciples' attention seems to be elsewhere: puzzling over why it says Elijah must come first. Whether this is because they have just seen Elijah talking with Jesus, or whether something else has provoked their memory of Malachi 4:5–6, we do not know. But they are thinking through what they know of the coming of God's kingdom.

Jesus has been teaching them that the events leading to the coming of the kingdom may look very different from what they have been expecting (Matthew 16:21–28). Here, he reiterates that he will die and be raised from the dead, identifying himself with the Son of Man of Daniel 7:13–14. But he drops the subject he started and talks through with them their own question. In verse 11, he seems to be quoting or summarising the expectation and then, in verse 12, he explains that this expectation has already been fulfilled, alluding to the life, ministry and death of John the Baptist. He also brings them back to the subject he started with, noting that his own fate will be the same as that of the Baptist.

But, at least as Matthew narrates it, only one penny drops. The piece of the puzzle that found its place was the prophecy around Elijah being fulfilled in John the Baptist. The rest had to wait for later. Sometimes, we can rush to share things which God in his good time will teach people. Sometimes, we can rush to learn things which God in his good time will teach us. None of us gets everything about Jesus first time around. This should not worry us. In time, the disciples became the most amazing witnesses to Jesus and brought many to faith. Today's reading should teach us a lesson in patience and trust.

5 A lesson in faith

Matthew 17:14–21

This passage bristles with difficulties. Matthew has Jesus identify an illness as caused by demonic possession. How we understand illness, exorcism and the relationship of the biblical language of spiritual warfare to contemporary life are but three of the vast areas this text might open up. But today I want to focus on its main theme: faith. We cannot get away from the fact that Jesus challenges his disciples, and all his hearers, to greater faith.

Note that Jesus' rebuke is aimed at people's lack of faith. Verse 20 makes the reason for the disciples' inability to cure the boy entirely clear: a lack of faith. His rebuke, 'you faithless and perverse generation' (v. 17), picks up on this – and there is nothing in the context to suggest what kind of waywardness Jesus has in mind except their lack of faith.

Jesus then comes out with the extraordinary statement that if they have faith the size of a mustard seed, they will be able to tell the mountain they have just come down to move and it will move. The context in Matthew does not allow us to explain the challenge away by using ancient myth (as we might with Mark 11:22–24). Nor can we explain it away by saying Jesus just wants us to have faith the size of a mustard seed – assuming he requires no more of us. That turns the punchline on its head. Jesus rebukes the disciples for having 'little faith' and urges them to grow their little faith so that it becomes the size of a mustard seed, because that way they will have enough faith to move the mountain. Moreover, Paul talks about mountain-moving faith (1 Corinthians 13:2). So, it seems that the early church was aware that Jesus spoke about mountain-moving faith and that this had become proverbial; Paul makes no attempt to explain it away. Even though few of us (unless we are building railways) are likely to want to move actual mountains, the challenge still remains: do we really trust that God can work miracles and are we willing to ask him to grant us or teach us such faith?

6 Another puzzle piece

The disciples' reaction is interesting. In the event of the resurrection, they seem to have been overjoyed. Mary and Mary Magdalene left the tomb with the news of Jesus' resurrection 'with fear and great joy' (Matthew 28:8). Although some doubted when they saw the risen Jesus, it seems most of the eleven disciples worshipped Jesus (Matthew 28:17). So why are they greatly distressed at the news that Jesus will rise again on the third day?

It seems that, again, not all the pieces of the puzzle are falling into place. The disciples appear to be falling into the same trap Peter fell into when Jesus first predicted these things (Matthew 16:21–23). Matthew does not record any of them voicing their thoughts this time around. However, they do not like what they hear. The thought of Jesus being betrayed and killed does not compute. It causes them grief and they respond accordingly. On the other hand, they do seem to understand what Jesus is saying and their response to the prediction of his suffering is understandable.

Sometimes God's ways are not easy to understand – even on the second retelling. When Jesus first gave them this news, he made it clear that 'it is necessary' (Greek: *dei*) for these things to happen. But the sheer distress of Jesus' suffering, perhaps also the confusion caused by someone who claimed to be the Messiah but was convinced he was going to die, was simply too much for them to take in and own. Sometimes, growing in faith can be like that. There are truths; Jesus has taught them. However, we find them unpalatable, so we ignore them or try to explain them away. Perhaps for many of us in the wealthier world, Jesus' words on the fate of the rich are like that. Perhaps for many of us in free countries, Jesus' words on persecution are like that. Whatever the words that cause us concern personally, the reactions of the disciples ought to be encouraging. They still followed him, listening and trying to learn. Perhaps Jesus' reaction ought to be even more encouraging. He never gave up on his disciples. Whoever followed him, he took seriously and, through all the ups and downs, he taught them the ways of God in truth and love.

Guidelines

Personal identity has become an incredibly important part of our culture. The major justice issues in our culture revolve around personal identity – and generally around the questions of how we identify ourselves in terms of our sex, gender, race, religion, culture or subculture. The current cultural norms are that our identities are sacrosanct and nobody has the right to challenge our identity. I wonder, also, whether we are creating a cultural myth in which we believe that our identities are not only sacrosanct but fixed in a way that means that not only can they not be challenged, but they cannot be changed either.

I sometimes feel I am living in a very different world from the world (or perhaps subculture) I grew up in. That was a world in which everybody seemed to challenge your identity and worldview and expected you to change it to fit their version of Utopia – particularly if you were a WASP (White Anglo-Saxon Protestant) male.

But even the most ardent of 1980s gender and race campaigners pale into insignificance when put alongside Jesus. In this week's readings, Jesus has driven a cart and horse through the worldview of his disciples – a worldview which was fundamental to their understanding of their identity as his disciples. The glorious vision of the kingdom is now replaced by his death and resurrection. The confusion has been so great that the disciples do not seem to hear the good news in the word 'resurrection'. Perhaps we tame Jesus too much in our retellings of his life and teaching. His vision is for a world transformed, the kingdom of peace and justice founded in the genuine love of all humanity for all humanity (which is tricky at the best of times), and won through his blood and, sometimes, our martyrdom. This vision can be as hard for us to take as it was for his first disciples. We may struggle to take it on board and to let it so sink through us that it forms our behaviours. But this is how Jesus longs to give us our new identity, our true identity, in him.

1 Generosity

Matthew 17:24–27

This funny little story seems a bit peculiar on first reading. So, it is probably worth explaining. The people who address Peter are those who collect the 'two drachmas' (Greek: *ta didrachma*) which is the exact amount of the temple tax – an annual tax collected to support the sacrificial system in the temple. It is probably no surprise that these people question Peter as to whether Jesus pays the tax, as Jesus had some stern warnings about the temple, not least that it would be destroyed (see Matthew 24:1–4). Despite the fact that Jesus saw his own death replacing the sacrificial system (see Matthew 26:26–29), Peter affirms that Jesus does pay the tax to support the sacrificial system. When they get home, Jesus asks Peter who Gentile rulers exact taxes from – their family or those outside their family. Peter gives the obvious answer. Then Jesus extrapolates from this that surely the sons of God (i.e. Israel, the people of God) should be free from the temple tax – hence his response, 'then the children are free' (v. 26). However, so as not to cause offence to the people collecting this tax (possibly because they already know Jesus sees the temple as ripe for destruction), Jesus commands Peter to pay the tax from a coin that he will find in a fish he is about to catch. The coin Peter will find is a *stater*, which was a coin worth four *drachmas* – exactly the sum needed to pay the temple tax for both of them.

We would be premature to draw any conclusions from this that Jesus was opposed to commands about giving, as he clearly teaches obedience to regulations about tithing (Matthew 23:23). So we cannot use this story to justify the idea that giving to the work of God (let alone the local church) is a purely voluntary matter on which Jesus does not teach. However, we do see Jesus teach a disciple the importance of supporting the institutions God has put in place, even when those institutions are not perfect and will be closed down by God within a few decades. In an increasingly 'performance-related generosity' culture, where individuals tend to decide for themselves whether they think their church is worth giving to, Jesus' example might give us all pause for thought.

2 Humility with a capital 'H'

Matthew 18:1–7

If there is anything we have learned from psychoanalysis in the last 100 years, it is probably the extraordinary capacity of people to want to exercise power and how that plays out in families, clubs and workplaces as much as the so-called 'corridors of power'. Our reading today suggests 'twas ever thus. The church is not (and never has been) devoid of people who would love to exercise power over others, and Jesus warns us all sternly against this. This is clear from his invitation to become like children. This invitation has nothing to do with developing a naïve and responsibility-free dependence on God as some kind of sugar-daddy who simply exists to bless us (as sometimes has been suggested). The point of becoming like children is developing humility. Jesus follows up his invitation to become like children in verse 3 by specifying how we become childlike – 'humble like this child' in verse 4. Children had no political rights. They were entirely powerless and so had no authority to engage in power games. The point of Jesus' call to his disciples is that we strip ourselves of any inclination to play power games – that, in all our dealings with others, we present ourselves as totally and transparently humble.

The reason for this is Jesus' vision for his community of disciples. He wants his church to be a place where the powerless are welcomed. His warnings in verses 6 and 7 underline this in triplicate. Not only are we to welcome the powerless into the community of faith but we are to ensure that they are able to grow in faith. We must not do or say things which prevent them from growing in faith. Jesus acknowledges that there will be times when people do things that cause others to stumble, but he makes very clear that there will be consequences for those who cause the stumbling. Far from his call to be like children divesting us of responsibility, it gives us all in the church great responsibility. But that responsibility does not come with great power; it comes with an invitation to powerlessness. Few things could be more counter-cultural. But when you are on the receiving end of such a welcome, few things prove to be quite so refreshing.

3 Tough stuff

Matthew 18:8–9

These two verses are shocking, on a plain reading of the text. Cutting off limbs and being thrown into hell make for uncomfortable reading. We might be tempted to reach for the bookshop app where we can buy a nice Christian paperback which reassures us that Jesus did not really mean these things and that we are safe, after all. But really, we ought to sit with the text, acknowledge that Matthew puts these verses on the lips of Jesus and try to take some time to listen to what they may be saying to us.

First, there probably is good reason to assume that Jesus is exaggerating when he mentions cutting off our hands and feet or tearing out our eyes. Jesus believed that there would come a day when all would rise again out of their graves, and the righteous would be rewarded with everlasting life while the wicked would be punished with eternal destruction (Matthew 25:31–46; compare Daniel 12:1–3). On that day, the righteous would receive resurrection bodies (Matthew 22:23–32). This belief, which Jesus shared with many of his Jewish contemporaries, was that people would be given new whole bodies on the day of resurrection (2 Maccabees 7:1–40). So, it is unlikely that Jesus envisages people spending eternity with the scars of cutting off body parts. More likely, Jesus uses a graphic image to make his point. Jesus often does this. We sometimes distort his teachings in our attempts to make Jesus seem acceptable. But Jesus even compares discipleship to crucifixion (the worst of Roman punishments). If you are ever disturbed by Jesus' teachings, it probably means you understand him.

But why would Jesus use such an image to make his point? Quite simply, because he cares about our holiness. He cares about our holiness because he wants us to be right with God and because of how our unholiness affects others. By setting bad examples, we knock people off the road of faith. By hurting people, we set them back in faith. Both these things destroy faith in the loving God who alone can give people life, both now and for eternity. Because we can get so absorbed in ourselves and forget others, sometimes we need a shocking reminder to put us right.

4 Caring for those God cares for

Matthew 18:10–14

Most of us know the parable of the lost sheep from the version in Luke 15:3–7, and we understand it to be about the joy in heaven over one lost sinner who repents and turns to God. Matthew does something different with this parable. He makes it about how we help the lost sinner stay in the fold after they have turned to God so that they do enter the kingdom on that great and glorious day when Jesus comes again.

The difference between Matthew and Luke's versions probably arises because Jesus most likely told his parables many times and in different ways to make various points.

The key to understanding the parable here is Jesus' opening statement to be careful not to look down on any of his disciples. Again, Jesus is warning us all against any high-and-mighty attitudes that make us feel or think we have the right to see others as beneath us in any way. God has a host of angels looking after his children (particularly the powerless). These angels have instant access to our heavenly Father, who will send his angels to make sure that all those who follow him (particularly the powerless) have his protection. God does this because he is like the good shepherd who looks after all his sheep – even the one who wanders off. God does not cut his losses and leave things at that. He does what is necessary to bring his wayward followers back into the fold. This is because God does not want a single one of those who have repented of their sins and turned to him to wander off and be lost to eternal punishment on the day God comes again to judge the world. Rather, God wants all who have tuned to him to enter his eternal kingdom.

In the context of Matthew 18, the parable becomes not simply an affirmation of the faithfulness of God but an admonition to all of us who belong to God. If God will take so much care over individual believers, how much more should we be careful to act in ways that help people to follow God and ensure that nothing we do or say puts them off track?

5 Like a Gentile or tax collector

There is no getting around the fact that this text is about church discipline. Even verse 20, 'for where two or three are gathered in my name, I am there among them', is about church discipline. We know that because it starts with the word 'for' (Greek: *gar*) which connects what follows to what has come before. What has come before outlines a stepped approach to discipline within the community (not entirely unlike the ACAS Code of Practice on Disciplinary and Grievance Procedures in its stepped approach to sorting out difficulties in relationships, for UK readers). This might come as a surprise to anyone used to hearing and quoting this verse at the start of a prayer meeting. But the meaning of the verse in context is actually remarkably good news.

As anyone in leadership (whether in the workplace, churches, community groups or within a family) knows, problems in relationships arise. People do bad things to each other. As Jesus puts it, 'If another member of the church (literally 'brother' [Greek: *adelphos*]) sins against you' (v. 15). When these things happen, we need to know how to handle them. Jesus teaches an approach which starts low-key but is willing to take things further in order to ensure that things are sorted out, but his overriding concern is that every opportunity is given to win the brother or sister back and effect repentance and reconciliation.

Interestingly, even 'let such a one be to you as a Gentile and a tax-collector' may not be quite as stern as it sounds. How did Jesus treat tax collectors? He called them to repentance and welcomed them into his family. How did he command his disciples to treat the Gentiles? In exactly the same way (Matthew 28:18–20). Compared to professional codes of practice (at least in the UK) where nobody expects dismissal to be followed by a permanent open-hearted willingness to welcome the dismissed back into the company, Jesus' procedure actually seems rather generous. But the really good news is that Jesus promises to be present with his people in all the heartache of church discipline. And as any compassionate leader knows, there is a lot of heartache in this – so Jesus' promise to be with us is incredibly encouraging.

6 The cost of grace

Matthew 18:21–35

In our autonomy-ridden culture, we can disapprove of Jesus' vision of a church culture where people hold us to account. We instinctively dislike the idea that anyone could discipline us – even Jesus. Peter, however, has a very different problem with Jesus from the one we have. He has listened to Jesus' teaching on community-building and decided that this is all rather costly. Loving the weaker Christian is good, but surely there are limits? When you give yourself, your time, your life to people who time and again let you down – surely there must be a limit? When the people who you help and invest so much of yourself in throw it all back in your face (as happens in Christian ministry), surely, we have the right to call time at some point? When they are unreliable, unkind, hurtful to your face and behind your back – surely, we do not have to let them walk all over us? Peter wants to know the limits to this attitude of grace, forgiveness and open-heartedness even to those beyond the pale.

Now, before we criticise Peter, let's put ourselves in his shoes. We know from the gospel that he will head up the church (Matthew 16:18). We know that even the twelve disciples play power games (Matthew 20:17–28). We know that the crowds that are supportive of Jesus one day, cry, 'Crucify him!' the next (Matthew 27:22–23). We have no right to criticise Peter unless we have been in church leadership and have gone through what lay ahead of him. The way some Christians act, being willing to forgive seven times, is remarkably generous. Unless we have been in Peter's position, we can scarcely begin to understand this well-known parable about the abounding grace and just severity of God. We need to place ourselves in the position of the slave who owed 10,000 talents while acknowledging the deepest hurts inflicted on us by our Christian brothers and sisters, and our own reactions to them. Otherwise, we reduce this parable to banality. But if we read it this way, we will surely be overcome once again by the grace of God.

Guidelines

Grace is costly. Many of us love to rejoice in the price that God paid on our behalf in Jesus' death on the cross, but are perhaps less inclined to be enthusiastic about the costly price of grace which we are called to pay as people committed to following Jesus as our Lord. Jesus has called each one of us to carry our cross if we would be his disciples, and so we cannot pretend that the life of faith is without cost. Any who try to write this out of Christian faith are simply attempting to reconstruct the illusions Jesus has been gently stripping away from the eyes of his disciples.

Jesus teaches them and us that the cost of grace does not stop with our inclusion in God's family. That is where we start to understand the cost and sometimes pay the price of a life of grace. God's new family in Christ is full of sinners. Forgiven sinners, but sinners nonetheless, who are, by and large, not fully reformed. The result is that we hurt each other and Jesus appears to be able to see this reality clearly in his instructions on community-building. Nonetheless, he does not start with how we can make sure that those responsible for hurting others make amends. He starts with an injunction to lay down our power, to become powerless like children and so unable to play power games. He calls us to a new reality of relationships where we are all on the same level. He calls us to be very careful that we steer well clear of doing or saying anything which might derail the faith of another believer. His warnings concerning this are pretty stark – giving us some idea of his passion for a community of believers who prioritise holiness in their own lives as a way of setting an example to each other and encouraging each other to grow as disciples. Jesus' words, 'Take care that you do not despise one of these little ones' (Matthew 18:10), encapsulate the care that he longs for us to take of each other and the respect that he longs for each of us to have towards each other – the same love and respect our heavenly Father has for each one of us.

Walking with the Judges: justice and mercy in the promised land (part II)

Isabelle Hamley

Judges is a little-loved book in the Bible. It seems strange, alien: characters are deeply flawed, violence and horror abound, and God often seems absent. Yet its themes are deeply contemporary too: leadership, the use and misuse of power, collective and individual responsibility, justice and mercy, gender relations, sexual and child abuse, individualism, greed, oppression, powerlessness… The themes are ones we recognise all too easily from today's headlines. So how can we read the book of Judges in ways that enable us to attend to the presence of God in the midst of the messiness and pain of real life?

First, reading Judges isn't about mining history, or seeking nuggets of teaching, but about listening to its prophetic challenge to the ways we live. Second, we find a clue in the name – 'Judges'. The Hebrew root translated as 'judges', *shophet*, also forms part of the Hebrew word for 'justice', *mishpat*. Judges is concerned with justice in the broadest sense, building a life that leaves behind the ways of thinking of Egypt and instead practises the ways of the Lord as outlined in the covenant at Sinai. But the people struggle; from the high optimism of the end of Joshua's life, the nation's practices deteriorate, individualism takes root and the common good recedes ever further. In this second half of the book, the narrative becomes darker and begs us to confront the worst aspects of human nature, and the impact of sin on the most vulnerable members of society.

Yet, within it all, Judges sows seeds of hope: the presence of Yahweh never recedes very far away, and in the midst of sin, brokenness and pain, God hears the pain of his people, and responds, though rarely in ways they recognise, desire or respond to.

Unless otherwise stated, Bible quotations are taken from the NRSV.

1 Who shall lead?

Judges 10:17—11:12

Halfway through Judges, we return to the question that opened the book: who shall lead? The answer in chapter 1 was: Judah. The people had great hopes, and Judah and Benjamin lead in entering the promised land. Some time later, there is little sense of Israel moving together as a nation. A tribe is being threatened, and they need to defend themselves. This time, there is no natural leader and the people do not ask God. Israel's walk with God is more distant already. The question of leadership lingers unanswered.

The writer then introduces Jephthah, a man of many contradictions: a 'mighty warrior', a description that suggests honour, status and recognition, and 'the son of a prostitute', disregarded, of uncertain parentage, run out of town by a resentful family. Jephthah reminds us of Abimelech: a rift with his brothers, moving away from home and taking up with outlaws. Yet Jephthah, here, is a victim: an unloved child, failed by both family and the wider community. The writer again sets the scene to highlight how sin and brokenness are transmitted and strengthened between generations, and prompts readers to ask: how is leadership shaped by both leader and community? How will these early experiences form Jephthah into the man he will become? How does injustice today prevent justice for tomorrow?

In desperation for a military chief, the elders of the town seek out Jephthah. But note their offer: previously, their leader was to be leader in peace as well as war, civic and community leader as well as war chief. But they only offer military leadership to Jephthah. Jephthah challenges them and highlights their utilitarian motives. They simply want to use him. The elders fail to apologise, but up their offer, and Jephthah accepts, with a caveat. He does not want leadership to simply be given; he wants to earn it, and thereby prove his worth. He is desperate to be accepted, and desperate to prove himself. This desire is stronger than any other impulse within him; he does not appear to act out of love of God or love for his country. He is trying to fill his inner void, to heal the pain of rejection. As both leader and man, his actions are shaped and defined primarily by his own fragility. The combination of a wounded leader who does not recognise his own vulnerability and weaknesses, and a harsh, utilitarian community, sets the scene for what is to come.

2 Power abused

Jephthah argues with the enemy king and prepares for battle. The Spirit falls on him and confirms the people's choice of leader. At this point, Jephthah would normally lead his army into battle. Instead, he does something quite extraordinary, and makes a strange vow to sacrifice whoever comes out of his house.

Why make the vow? Victory has already been sealed through the giving of the Spirit. God has not asked for anything from Jephthah. But Jephthah, once again, is keen to be in control and prove himself. He refuses a free gift and tries to 'buy' the Lord's favour. The words of his vow are alarming: in the ancient world, women usually greeted returning warriors by coming out of houses with music and dancing. Jephthah knew exactly what he was promising, in either ignorance or contradiction of the biblical prohibition of human sacrifice. It is his own interest and desire for honour that shapes his actions.

When his daughter comes out, he shows no surprise and reproaches her for causing him sorrow. It never seems to occur to him that he could choose not to sacrifice her, regardless of the cost to his honour; or turn to God or scripture for advice – Leviticus sets a price to pay to redeem the life of a vowed human being. There was never any spiritual need for Jephthah to kill his daughter. When the needs of individuals dominate, those with less power and status suffer. The gradual obliteration of women, as more vulnerable in a patriarchal society, is picking up pace. The community who had failed Jephthah as a child now fails his daughter by staying silent.

The young woman's last wish is to go away and mourn with her friends, gathered together in a community of the vulnerable. Whereas her father and the men of Gilead destroy community, the young woman gathers it, and the community in turn sets up a practice of resistance. They remember. Without them, Jephthah would be remembered as a straightforward hero. With their lament and testimony, the reality of women's lives is acknowledged, and Jephthah's pursuit of honour and power exposed for what it is. The writer chooses not to dwell on the details of the sacrifice; he eschews a voyeuristic description and dwells instead on the picture of an alternative community, drawn together through lament and opposition.

3 A new hope?

Jephthah's rule proceeds, ushered in horror with the death of his daughter, and widens in brutality to tribes that do not recognise his leadership. As a leader, his self-centredness and inner brokenness drive Israel further from the Lord's commands. Israel does not hold him accountable, does not challenge him and moves further away from God. The cycle repeats itself: the people sin, God withdraws, they find themselves oppressed. But this time, Israel does not cry out in pain or ask for deliverance. Their minds are now so fully captive to Canaan that they do not recognise or want to escape from their new condition. In effect, they have returned to a state similar to their slavery in Egypt.

God, however, has not forgotten, and when the people fail to cry, he takes the initiative. God sends a messenger who proclaims a hope that Israel was not looking for. He appears to Manoah's wife in a classic annunciation scene: the mother is said to be barren, the boy (always a boy) will be special in the destiny of Israel. The angel's instructions are clear: the boy will be a Nazirite, bound by law and custom, as described in Numbers 6:1–21. Yet there is a shadow in the message. The boy will only 'begin to deliver' (v. 5).

Manoah himself is not impressed that his wife was the sole recipient of the revelation. He muscles in and demands an apparition of his own. The lack of trust, together with the woman's namelessness, highlights how far the position of women has deteriorated since Achsah and Deborah at the beginning of the book. The angel pushes back against Manoah's demands and once again, appears to the woman. When Manoah, thanks to his wife, finally does meet the angel, he struggles to recognise the divine messenger for what he is. He insists on offering the 'man' the type of offering that should only be offered to God, and the angel gently, but firmly, corrects him: 'if you want to prepare a burnt-offering, then offer it to the Lord.'

Manoah and his wife seem to understand part of the story of God, but they are not practised in relating to God. Manoah in particular fails to recognise God at work and the spiritual wisdom of his wife. When the people walk away from God, each generation in succession loses a little more knowledge and experience of God, so that gradually, the people no longer know, recognise or discern God, or their own need of God.

4 One wedding, many funerals

Now we meet Israel's promised deliverer, Samson. Reader expectations are great, given the circumstances of his birth. As soon as 'adult' Samson is introduced, a recurrent stress on what Samson *sees* begins. In chapter 13, the narrator stressed what his mother could see, and how the couple came to see God in the fire. Now, Samson *sees* a girl and wants her – even though she belongs to the nation oppressing Israel. In a book that repeatedly stresses that 'Israel did evil in the eyes of the Lord' and 'each man did what was right in his own eyes', this focus on sight is a clue for the reader to think metaphorically and be alert to the pattern of Samson's life. Will he, like others, decide for himself what is 'right in his own eyes', regardless of what is right in the eyes of the Lord? Individualism and the individualisation of morality are at the heart of sinful choices in Judges.

Samson was a Nazirite. He should stay away from grape products, but chooses to go into a vineyard. He should stay ritually clean and avoid dead bodies, but kills a lion with his bare hands. He then chooses to return and eat what came out of the carcass. He should be leading Israel to God, but shares unclean food with his parents, without telling them. Samson shows little regard for his heritage or calling and breaks every aspect of his Nazirite status. Unlike Jephthah, who was wounded, but tried, Samson goes his own way, the way he sees fit.

He wilfully ignores his mother's advice, so that as a woman and a person with spiritual wisdom, she is silenced and erased from the story of the deliverer. Instead, this young man is left, alone, despite Philistine 'companions' (or is it guards?) set around him. He forces his young bride into the impossible position of choosing between her fiancé and her family. When he is outsmarted by the Philistines, instead of yielding with good grace, he erupts with anger, kills bystanders and leaves the woman behind. The narrator is forced to conclude that if this is the deliverer, then God must be acting despite Samson, rather than with Samson. The deliverer himself is unable to see where God is leading. He wants to unite with the prevalent culture, rather than lead the people away from it. God is acting alone for an Israel who ignores and rejects him.

5 Mimicking the Philistines

Samson continues to exhibit astonishing self-centredness and immaturity. The story of his wife is often glossed over, the young woman's life forgotten. Samson had initiated a cycle of disproportionate violence and retaliation with the murder of 20 random Philistines. Yet he does not appear to understand the impact of his actions, as he goes back into Philistine territory and expects his 'wife' to welcome him. The young woman never speaks for herself. At every step of the story, she is controlled by the men around her. Whether in Israel or Philistia, the treatment of women is spiralling out of control as the men do what is right in their own eyes and seek their own interest.

Samson is indiscriminate in his violence – he brutalises the natural world as much as the human world; the destruction of crops is a deadly blow to survival, while destroying vineyards and olive groves annihilates years of patient work. In this story, the Philistines are brutal too, but they appear more restrained: they only attack targets connected to Samson, or Samson himself. In return, he attacks and believes himself justified. Readers are forced to ask, what is justice here? Both Samson and the Philistines invoke justice and just deserts, with no difference in their use of the words, yet their justice causes more injustice than was present beforehand. Justice is central to the book of Judges: aside from Yahweh's commandments, it becomes misshapen, twisted by individuals' choices, biases and brokenness.

Samson is supposed to be a judge, yet he does little to usher in the kind of justice that brings about peace, general prosperity and the respect of every person made in the image of God. The further away from Yahweh the people move, the more 'justice' is made in their own image and used to justify the brutalisation of the more vulnerable – in this story, women and animals.

Unsurprisingly, Israel fails to recognise Samson as their judge, and instead sees him as a threat. The man meant to be Israel's deliverer is instead bound by Judah and handed over to the Philistines. Neither Israel nor Samson is able to discern their vocation to social distinctiveness and Yahweh worship, let alone act on it. And yet, when Samson proclaims himself as victor and deserving praise, God still opens the rock and gives him water, underlying that the basis of God's love for Israel is grace, not 'just deserts'.

6 Dying with the Philistines

Judges 16:4–31

As a Nazirite supposed to stay away from grape products, Samson once again goes to an area known for its vineyards. He is expected to avoid dead bodies, but kills repeatedly. He is called to embody Israel's distinctiveness, but behaves just like the Philistines, and consistently pursues Philistine women. The only sign left from his Nazirite identity is his hair.

But he falls in love with Delilah – a mysterious woman, whose ethnicity is unknown, and whose living arrangements do not fit recognisable patterns. He seems oblivious to the political background, to Israel's bondage and to the Philistines' determination to capture him. All that interests Samson is Samson, and he treats God's gifts as his possession, rather than as a vocation. As Delilah makes it clear that she is after his secret, he shows little fear and thinks himself invincible. Samson seems to think that he is special, and that his special powers reside not in interaction with God, or in God's grace, but in himself. When finally he gives up his secret, he does not lose strength magically, but breaks the last vestige of the Nazirite vow that shaped his life. Samson's relationship with God has dwindled to nothing, and he is left as he is: an irresponsible, arrogant man-child to be captured by his enemies.

Samson, who roamed wherever he wanted, is tethered and jailed. Samson, who epitomised violent, destructive masculinity, is put to grinding at the mill, a task usually performed by animals or women. Samson, whose eyes consistently led him astray, who did what was right in his own eyes, loses his eyes.

Yet the Philistines are no different: in their arrogance and ruthlessness, they seek to humiliate Samson further. Samson is finally conscious of his own powerlessness and dependence on God. His hair has started to grow again, but that does not give him strength, so, finally, he turns to God and prays. It is a selfish prayer – he wants revenge. But it is prayer nonetheless, and as the Philistines drink to their gods, the God of Israel comes alongside his people, despite their indifference and misdirected wishes, and the Philistine leadership is eradicated.

Samson is buried with his ancestors, united with the people whose company he avoided his entire life. Just like Samson, Israel is losing its distinctiveness and threatening to be absorbed into the culture of their oppressors. For Israel to survive, God will have to act miraculously, independently, in grace and compassion.

Guidelines

The second half of Judges continues the deteriorating spiral in the life of Israel. Instead of the Judges ushering in a time of peace, when people and land have rest, they usher in horror and abuse (Jephthah) and create opportunities for self-centred skirmishes that lead to additional suffering for the entire people (Samson). With both Samson and Jephthah, we continue to see an accelerating pattern of self-centredness in leaders; instead of leading on behalf of the people, they seek personal gain, and forget that they were called by God, not because they were special, not for their own benefit, but called to walk with God to lead Israel into the justice and peace that was promised to those who had come out of Egypt.

Their example is of course dramatic; and yet, how easy is it today to forget that God's gifts, God's Spirit, God's blessings and calling are always meant to benefit others. The people of Israel were not called to enjoy blessing for their own sake, they were called to be a blessing to the nations. Their distinctiveness was not meant to be a badge of honour, but an invitation into a way of life shaped by justice, mercy, compassion and grace. When we hoard blessings and gifts, we forget our calling in the world.

- How do we keep our eyes on what we are called to as communities?
- What kind of distinctiveness are we called to exhibit?
- What blessings do we have, as individuals, churches and nations, and what is God calling us to do with them?

1 Topsy-turvy worship

Judges 17

Judges 17 marks a shift in the story of Judges. There are no obvious, named leaders anymore. The camera has shifted from its focus on leadership to an 'every person' perspective, and we are invited to observe how domestic life and public life mirror each other. First, in the story of Micah (17) and the story of Dan (18), then in the story of one, nameless couple (19) and the life of Israel as a whole (20—21). These last few chapters all belong together, united by the refrain, 'In those days, there was no king in Israel; all the people did what was right in their own eyes.' Until now, the people did 'what was evil in the eyes of the Lord'. At least there is a recognition of what was evil, and that evil is measured by God. But even this is now disintegrating. The Lord is no longer king in Israel, and the people no longer use God's definition of right and wrong: everyone makes up right and wrong for themselves. As a result, any notion of common good and common values disintegrates, and the nation falls into anarchy.

First, here in Judges 17, we meet a man, Micah, and his mother. In direct defiance of the ten commandments, Micah not only steals, but steals from his mother, thereby breaking two laws at once. His mother, meanwhile, curses the thief. Micah has a change of heart and tells his mother about the theft; she passes no judgement, does not hold him responsible and blesses him instead. This is not justice, and neither is it grace. She simply ignores his actions, and he does not repent.

Neither seems concerned with doing right. Both seem utterly confused about how to do right. The mother consecrates the money to *the Lord*, but uses it to make an idol! Micah, meanwhile, has a shrine of his own and makes his own priest. Israel had a system of authorised ministry, through priests and Levites, charged with showing the ways of the Lord. Micah ignores Israel's shared heritage, worship and life shaped by its history and God's teaching. Instead, he gets his own priest, whom he can shape. There is very little sense of Israel as the whole people of God here. Religion has become a way to ensure prosperity, rather than reflecting the patient, transformative walk with God that Israel was called to. Faith and ethics have been emptied of content, emptied of God and replaced with individual desires and powerplay.

2 Worship and justice entwined

The next part of the story unfolds as a delegation from the tribe of Dan comes north to find land. Notice the change from the beginning, when the tribes were given an inheritance. Inheritances cannot be taken, only given. But Dan seeks to find land for themselves, rather than accept what was given by God. They then send out some young men to spy out the land, in a sad parody of the beginning of Joshua and spies sent to Jericho. Here, the city they look at is described repeatedly as quiet and secure, prosperous and peaceful. What a contrast to the lying, warlike, aggressive tribe! Unlike in earlier conquest narratives, the inhabitants are not described as unjust, idolatrous or even resisting. Dan simply slaughters innocent people, without any directive from God – for land not allotted to them – and turns it into a centre of idolatry. The narrator draws our attention to the fate of the city through repeated description of its inhabitants, and by reminding us of its former name. Everywhere else, when a city is conquered, we are told, 'this was its name, and from now on, it is called X'. Here the formula is reversed, and the narrator stresses the former, rather than the latter name. It is quite clear that the Danites' actions are not an example of covenantal living.

It is little surprise, then, that the interlude at the house of Micah should proceed as it does. The man who had stolen from his own mother finds that he is now dispossessed. The man who had eluded consequences for his own actions finds that Dan can steal from him with impunity. The man who had trusted in idols finds that his idols can be co-opted by anyone who comes by. And the young man who had accepted serving a well-paying master rather than be faithful to his calling as a Levite has no qualms about serving a well-paying tribe with its own idols. In a nation where everyone does what is right in his own eyes, there is no recourse in the face of injustice, theft and brutality. To do justice requires a shared commitment to norms and behaviour that benefit the community. Individualism and a spiritual pick-and-mix approach destroy this sense of shared value and the protections that come with them. In this new Israel, everyone is vulnerable.

3 At this time, there was no king

Judges 19:1–26

Judges 19 opens the final set of stories to conclude the book of the Judges. Once again, the narrator reminds us, at the outset, that there is no king. No overall, supreme authority. People do what they want. They decide what is right. In this uncertain world, a young woman crosses Israel alone, on foot, to get away from her mate – the text calls him husband, but she is only a 'concubine', without the rights and protections of a married woman. The man is a Levite, supposed to lead people to God, yet once again, this Levite seems disconnected from communities of faith and worship. The young woman never speaks, and we do not know her name. She looks for the protection of her father, but when her husband comes after her, the men forget her. After days of feasting, her husband makes the unwise decision to leave late in the day, when travelling becomes more dangerous. They break their journey in Gibeah, which he deems safer because it is an Israelite town. Ironically, staying away from an Israel that has departed from God's law would have been safer.

No one treats them as kin, as fellow-Israelites, as they wait in the public square. Only an old man, a stranger himself, takes them in. The normal rules of hospitality and friendship have broken down before they even get inside. As Israel breaks down into ever smaller units – tribes, clans, families, individuals – kinship and interdependence are lost. The Levite and his family are treated as strangers, viewed with suspicion and distrust. Once people are seen as 'other', as not belonging, it is a short step to treating them as less than human, not deserving of the same dignity and care as those who are 'like us'. Here in Gibeah, some 'wicked men' surround the house and threaten the Levite, intending to humiliate and violate him, reinforcing the sense that he does not belong, that he is not one of them. The old man puts up a little resistance, and proposes what he sees as a solution: why not brutalise young women, who are even more 'other'? They belong even less, have fewer rights. He appeals to their common identity as men to deflect the threat on to someone else. The Levite does not even wait for the end of the negotiations and simply throws his concubine out to the mob. The story is told economically, without voyeuristic details. Readers are simply left with the image of the brutalised young woman teetering towards the house where the men are safely barricaded. They do not seek help, go to look for her or even wait up for her. They do not open the door to let her in, and she collapses on the threshold. Those indoors have bought their safety at her expense, and sleep soundly on it.

4 Justice and truth

As readers, we are privy to the concubine's fate. Meanwhile, those inside are carrying on as normal: the Levite gets up and gets ready to go. Earlier in the story, we were told that he went after his concubine to 'speak tenderly to her' (19.3). He does not speak to her in the chapter until now. She lies on the threshold, unable to move, and he orders her to get up. His callousness is obviously meant to shock. He does not check her, see whether she can be helped, tend to her wounds. He simply hoists her on a donkey and goes. The book of Judges opened with another story of a woman's journey: Achsah left her husband temporarily, riding a donkey, to go and demand good land from her father – and was blessed. This woman left her husband and returned to her father, but received no blessing, and returns home slung across a donkey like cargo. The men of the city, and now the Levite, have dehumanised her, and now, when he gets home – home being normally a place of safety – he dismembers her like an animal, without ever checking she was dead.

Just like chapters 17—18, this story now moves from the local and domestic to the communal and national. The Levite uses her body as a call to arms – though the message is unclear. As a Levite, he was a religious leader, supposed to lead the people in justice and holiness. But his speech to the nation only has the appearance of a call for justice. He carefully edits the story: he says the men of Gibeah wanted to kill, rather than rape, him; instead of a few wicked men, they become 'the lords of Gibeah'; instead of the concubine coming home to a household that threw her out in the first place, then did not let her back in, he says the men of Gibeah 'raped [her] until she died' (v. 5). He calls for justice, yet does not present the truth. The tribes of Israel now gathered do not seek out the truth, either, nor do they turn to their own laws and statutes to discern what the right response may be. They do ask Benjamin for an explanation, but the tribe of Benjamin simply stands with their own, without seeking truth or justice either. The Levite's call to arms plays on tribal identities, prejudices and divisions, and instead of doing justice, the nation descends into civil war.

5 Battle against the Lord

Israel proceeds to battle against Benjamin, cast as the enemy, the 'other', whose actions are unthinkable, un-Israelite: 'Has such a thing ever happened since the day that the Israelites came up from the land of Egypt until this day?' (19:30) The question summarises the situation. Benjamin is seen as doing something that goes against everything that Israel is as a nation. Never mind Abimelech, Jephthah or Samson. Israel excuses its own history but demonises Benjamin. The murdered, violated woman disappears as a person whose fate demands justice and becomes a pretext for war. Meanwhile, there is a shift in the nation's self-understanding. Normally they recall their history as 'the day the Lord brought you/us out of Egypt'. But now, in this Israel with no king, God is taken out and Israel becomes the author of its own salvation.

As Israel goes to battle, there is a pale echo of Judges 1, asking God who should lead. In Judges 1, battle was mandated by God, aimed at securing a place to live beyond the desert, and against the much stronger armies of the land. Here, battle is chosen by Israel, against Israel, by all the tribes against one, in an act of disproportionate retaliation. The tribes enquire of God, but they do not ask *whether* they should go to war in the first place, only *how* they should fight to ensure victory: they no longer see God as their king, let alone as partner in their history. God has become a cosmic insurance plan, a tribal God whom they seek to harness to underwrite their own plans. They do not try and listen, or seek counsel, and are no longer shaped by the teachings of either law or history. God is simply co-opted for their own aims.

War in Israel was not a free-for-all: there were rules of engagement set out in the law. War leading to the extermination of the enemy is highly restricted and specific, never to be used against Israel apart from the one instance of a town that has completely fallen into apostasy, after a thorough enquiry. Here, Israel exterminates an entire tribe, for the misdeeds of a few men in Gibeah, with no judicial process. In the entire book of Judges, we only see Israelites being killed by other Israelites. It is not Canaanites that are Israel's greatest threat – it is Israel itself, when they forget their calling and identity as the people of God.

6 Everyone did what was right in his own eyes

Chapter 21 makes a bad situation worse. Israel now regrets their actions, but get themselves in a muddle over yet another unwise vow. Jephthah had made a personal vow that resulted in the death of one person. Now Israel as a whole makes vows that will result in the deaths of hundreds of innocent civilians. Not only have they decimated Benjamin, but they have made it impossible for survivors to be reintegrated into the nation through the normal practices of marriage, through which bonds of kinship and interdependence are created. Because they regret what they did, they (ironically) turn against the one town who did not participate in the war and decide to kill them all (will they regret this, too?), aside from any women available for marriage, who will be forcibly taken and given to the Benjaminite men. The men who had gone to war to punish a few men for one rape, now sanction forced marriage, hence forced sexual relations, for hundreds of women. The nation as a whole mirrors and repeats what had been done by a few in Gibeah. Brutalised women are forced to marry brutalised men, within a context of war and violence that embeds pain and trauma into the very fabric of the nation. The first king of Israel, Saul, will be a Benjaminite. If we follow the logic of the story, he is the descendant of one of the surviving Benjaminites and one of the forcibly taken women.

The destruction of Jabesh-Gilead and its inhabitants proves insufficient to furnish Benjamin with all the 'brides' they need. Now Israel gives up any pretence of war and justice, and simply sanctions an attack on a group of women out celebrating a festival to the Lord in Shiloh, so that Benjamin can abduct the women they need. It is the elders of Israel who formulate the plan: the brutalisation of women is no longer isolated or linked to 'wicked men'; it is officially sanctioned and condoned by the leaders of the nation. Neither women nor men are seen or presented as individuals; they become means to an end, pawns that can be used or discarded at will. In a nation where everyone does what is right in their own eyes, there are no systems of justice or law, no prevailing norms or ethic that enable individuals to be protected. Ironically, Judges tells us that individualism results in nothing but the death of individuals.

Guidelines

The end of Judges is not for the faint-hearted. It turns your stomach and makes you wonder, why is this story even being told? It is a story of vulnerability, brutalisation and massacre. It is the kind of story that tells us that reading scripture isn't about escaping from the world, but about confronting the reality that our world is deeply, profoundly broken. The stories of chapters 19—21 are not unusual; they are repeated in many ways today, at home and abroad. To have them told in our scriptures tells us that even the most atrocious aspects of our humanity belong to the story of God's dealings with humanity, that there is nothing so awful that it cannot be brought in honesty before God. They also tell us that God does not always intervene, and that sometimes human actions lead to unspeakable evil and disaster. We need these stories in scripture, because they are our stories too. They are the stories of today's victims, who also cry out and get no answer. And if we feel uncomfortable reading them in scripture, then what does this ask of us about the world in which we live?

It would be easier to forget these stories, to skip these passages, just as it would be easier to close our eyes to the violence and brutalisation that our world inflicts on children, women and men. Their presence in scripture, however, is a gift: it is a mirror that tells the truth; a witness to the pain of victims, and a call to examine our communities deeply and honestly. Do we make space for today's stories to be told? Do we talk of times when God seems absent? And, more crucially, do we invite God to transform them so they become part of his unending story of hope, grace and redemption?

FURTHER READING

Robert Alter, *Ancient Israel: The former prophets: Joshua, Judges, Samuel and Kings* (W. W. Norton & Company, 2013).

Daniel I. Block, *The New American Commentary: An exegetical and theological exposition of holy scripture: Judges, Ruth – Vol. 6* (B&H Publishing, 1999).

Mercedes L. García Bachmann, *Wisdom Commentary: Judges* (Liturgical Press, 2018).

Isabelle Hamley, *God of Justice and Mercy: A theological commentary on Judges* (SCM, 2021).

Barry G. Webb, *The New International Commentary on the Old Testament: The book of Judges* (Eerdmans, 2012).

Romans 5—8: running with Romans

Stephen Finamore

In the opening chapters of his letter, Paul has set out the foundations of his argument. After his initial remarks, he presents his big idea – the righteousness of God. He means that the whole of creation is being put back on track because, through the life, death and resurrection of the Messiah Jesus, God has begun the process of keeping all his ancient promises. This is the message that Paul calls the 'gospel'. The disobedience of humankind and its consequences had derailed everything and, if Paul or his readers looked around for people who were living as God intended, their search would be in vain. Paul insists that this is true for every category of human, whether Jewish or Gentile. To address the issue, God sent his Son, Messiah Jesus, to be a 'mercy seat'. The seat, in the ancient Holy of Holies in the heart of the temple, was both the site of God's own presence and the site of the presentation of sacrifice. Paul understood that some people would struggle with the idea that God was fulfilling his promises in this way, because it seems to have no place for the law/Torah, that God had given to his people. However, Paul insists that, if you read it carefully, the law itself anticipates the gospel he is called to proclaim.

The opening verse of chapter 5 tells us what Paul believes he has demonstrated in his letter up to this point. He says, 'Therefore, since we are justified by faith…' To be justified means to become part of the people of God, which in turn means to be the part of humanity in which all God's promises find fulfilment, and this group can know, in the present, that God will find in their favour when the final judgement comes. The faith that Paul mentions is not simply intellectual assent to an idea or to a statement; it is a relational term that can be expressed using words like belief, trust, faithfulness, loyalty and allegiance.

Over the next four chapters, Paul will spell out how Messiah Jesus has undone the consequences of human disobedience, talk about the part the law has played in the story and then discuss what it means to belong to the Messiah. This will lead to a reflection on the way that life under the law leads to inner conflict, and about how this is resolved by God through the work of Jesus and the presence of God's Spirit in his people. This action does not affect people alone but through them it impacts the whole of the cosmos. All this means that those who follow Jesus can have complete confidence in God's love for them.

Unless otherwise stated, Bible quotations are taken from the NRSV.

1 Spelling things out

Romans 5:1–11

Those who are justified are those who are loyal to Messiah Jesus. This means that they are no longer in rebellion against God's purposes and so are at peace with him. One consequence of this is that they have the prospect of becoming what God intended when he first made humans – sharers of his glory (Psalm 8:5–6). All this puts any present suffering into perspective so that it can be understood as something that God uses to help his people to develop. They can do this because they experience the work of the Holy Spirit, who pours God's love into their inner lives.

In verse 6, Paul explains that the Messiah died for those on the wrong path. Stories circulated in the Roman world about people who chose to give their own lives for others. They tended to be motivated by the outstanding character of the other person. Nobody would dream of doing this for an enemy or for someone who ought to be held in contempt. But the gospel doesn't work like that. Instead, Messiah Jesus gave his life for those who opposed him, so that they would no longer have to face God's judgement. In other words, those who were once in opposition have been reconciled.

In the film *Saving Private Ryan*, a group of soldiers all give their lives to rescue Ryan, a young soldier caught behind enemy lines. The leader of the group, as he lies dying, tells Ryan to 'earn this'. He wanted to feel that Ryan would be worthy of his sacrifice. The film then shifts many years into the future, to a scene in a military cemetery where Ryan, now mature and with his family, stands before the grave of his rescuer. He summons his wife and asks her if he has been a good man – he wants to be reassured that he has been worthy of what was done for him. It's a poignant moment. But Paul's point is that God's love is so great that the Messiah died for sinners – for the unworthy – and that's even more amazing.

2 Back to the very beginning

Romans 5:12–17

The first humans rejected the purposes for which God created them even though they had been told that the consequences of such disobedience would be death (Genesis 2:17). The result of this was that the humans were no longer on a trajectory leading to glory, honour (as in Psalm 8:5) and life, but were heading instead in a very different direction. Being opposed to God and to his purposes is a condition that Paul calls 'sin', the outcome of which is spiritual death. When God gave his people the law – the Torah – it became evident that sin was the condition in which humans find themselves. Prior to the law, people may have been aware that something was amiss, but they would not have been able to define it. So, in the period between Adam, the first human and Moses, through whom God gave the law, death was in charge, even for those who had no idea they were breaking any rules – or that there were any rules to break. Nevertheless, there was hope. God never gives up and he planned to put people back on track. If a human had sent things in the wrong direction, then another human would have to put them right again. Therefore, the promised rescuer would be a type or counterpart to the primal human.

Adam broke a known rule and it resulted in death. Through the obedience of his counterpart, the Messiah, God gave a gift of grace. Adam and the Messiah are types of one another, but they cannot really be compared. The first brought judgement and condemnation, but the latter, even after lots of people had broken known rules, enabled people to be acquitted on all charges and become part of God's community. Adam rejected God's way of being human and brought death upon all that followed, whereas Messiah Jesus fully obeyed God's way, and those who trust him will be treated as though they have done the same. This means they will share his life in which he reigns as king. In one sense Adam and the Messiah are counterparts, but in another sense the consequences of their actions are so different that they shouldn't really be compared at all.

Ponder the idea that God refuses to give up on his purposes. What might this mean for us?

3 From death to life

Here's the pattern: Adam's disobedience led to all humanity finding itself outside of God's purposes, and hence under judgement, alienated from God and experiencing death. But the faithful obedience of Messiah Jesus, even to the point of death, leads to humans being brought back into God's purposes – to acquittal, community and life. When the human prototype crossed a line, the outcome was that the whole of humanity ended up in sin, the condition in which they oppose God's purposes. On the other hand, the outcome of Jesus' faithful obedience is that many are now being empowered to start to fulfil God's original purposes.

What part did the law play in all this? Well, those who knew the law knew where the lines were. As a result, they knew when they crossed those lines. Therefore, more than any other group of people, they were aware of the presence of sin, of living in opposition to God's purposes. The law has the effect of taking a magnifying glass to sin. Nevertheless, where this happened – which was in Israel, the only nation that knew God's law – grace was all the more apparent too. Where sin was reigning and producing death, grace came and through Messiah Jesus reigned in an obedience to God's purposes – the ones that produce life.

You could say that the law works like a doctor who makes a diagnosis. The patient already knows there's a problem but can't put a name to it. The doctor can see the nature of the problem and its root cause. All humans have a problem, and many are aware that something is amiss, but they need the law because it defines the problem and, if you read it carefully, promises the remedy. If you had no idea how things were supposed to be, you wouldn't know that the status quo wasn't the natural, intended condition of humanity. Messiah Jesus is God's cure for the condition that the law reveals.

In some ways this can be compared to the way that the law ought to work in any nation. When a law is broken this should reveal that an injustice has been done. The law should then also promise a remedy so that justice can be restored.

4 Baptism helps answer the questions

Romans 6:1–4

Paul brings in an imaginary discussion partner to make a point often made by those opposed to his arguments. This person claims that Paul is making sin sound like a good thing because it provides a context in which grace can abound. This would mean that those who followed Paul's teaching should remain in a condition of sin to enable grace to flourish. Paul, of course, rejects the idea completely. Those who follow Messiah Jesus have been transferred from one realm to another; they have died and have been reborn. They are no longer in the condition called 'sin' and so should no longer live as though they are opposed to God's purposes.

This transfer from death to life is signalled when people are baptised. In baptism, Jesus' followers are so identified with him that the things that are true of him are also true of them. He died and was buried and rose again. His followers are buried in the water and then rise to a new kind of life. Paul is not saying that this means that those who follow Jesus never sin; rather, he is saying that such disobedience is not appropriate to who they now are or to who they are becoming.

The apostle seems to be arguing that the baptised have a new identity or even a new mode of being and that certain ways of living belong to this and others do not.

5 The Christian has crossed over – and should live like it

Romans 6:5–14

Paul wants his readers to understand what has happened to them and how this affects who or what they have become. Some of the things that are true of the Messiah are also true of them. They have been joined to Jesus in his death and will be joined to him in his resurrection. In this new way of being, sin is no longer their boss and they no longer have to obey it. Death was the outcome of sin, but Jesus now lives a life that is free from the threat of death. The same is true for those who belong to him. Their lives are no longer in the realm of death and therefore no longer in the realm of sin. Instead, their lives are oriented towards God.

If you move to another country, you might decide to speak a new language, embrace a new culture and learn to obey a different system of laws. If this was your decision, then, every day, you would need to commit yourself to these new ways of living. Occasionally, you might find yourself speaking your native language, behaving according to your former cultural norms or instinctively obeying the old legal system by, for example, driving on the wrong side of the road. You would have to constantly remind yourself who you now are and where you now are, and then live accordingly. Over the years, these things become easier. Those who follow Jesus are called to live as God originally intended humans to live. They have moved to a new territory where things are done differently. Fortunately, as we shall see, they do not do this alone. They have the community of others who follow Jesus with them and, most importantly, they have the presence in their inner lives, of God's Holy Spirit.

6 An illustration from slavery

Romans 6:15–23

The use of the institution of slavery to make a spiritual point strikes our generation as awkward, or even offensive. However, Paul is certainly not endorsing slavery; he is simply using an illustration that would have been familiar to his original readers. He brings in his imaginary conversation partner again to ask a question. What basis can there be for ethics if we no longer obey the Torah? Without the law, what's to stop us doing wrong? Paul explains that, like enslaved people, all humans, whether they're aware of it or not, have an owner to whom they are obedient. And just as a slave can only have one owner, so can any human. Our owner was sin, and this led inevitably to wrongdoing and to death. However, the new owner is righteousness – the way of living that God intended when he first made humans – which leads to holiness and to life. Those who follow Jesus belong to God and so must be obedient to God by living in accordance with his purposes.

Every way of life has its consequences. In the end, they all boil down to two options. You can either belong to sin, where the outcome will be death, or you can belong to God and the result will be life. Those who follow Jesus are those who belong to God. Bob Dylan used to sing a song called 'Gotta Serve Somebody' that captures the basic idea of these verses. He set out the options that there are for every category of person – it may be the devil or it may be the Lord, but you gotta serve somebody. We humans, especially those in the contemporary west, like to think of ourselves as being free and making our own choices independently of the influences around us. Paul suggests that we are kidding ourselves. The truth is that humans always belong to, and are always in the service of, a spiritual reality.

Guidelines

Paul has explained the work of Jesus in terms of the story of Adam. It's as though God had set humans off on tracks that would lead them to share his glory. However, we refused to follow those tracks and instead built our own that went in the opposite direction. To make things worse, we found a way to turn the rails of the original tracks into a tangle of knots so that no one could follow them. Messiah Jesus untangled the knots and relaid the track and followed it to its destination and invited others to come after him. Those who trust in him find themselves back on the right tracks.

- Jesus has helped dig us out of a hole of our own making. Can you think of anyone, perhaps at work or at college, who helped you out of a situation you'd got yourself into? Does this help illustrate what Jesus has done?

- Do Paul's words about baptism suggest anything about the appropriateness of different baptismal traditions? If we follow his thinking at this point, who are the appropriate candidates and what is the appropriate mode of baptism? And do these things matter?

- One way to understand the Jewish law is to see it as revealing the human condition so that we recognise our need. Was there something or someone that prompted you to recognise that you needed God's grace and forgiveness?

- Think again about the idea of living in another country and adopting its ways. What's the hardest change to make? Compare this to living as a follower of Jesus. What changes do you most struggle with?

- Paul insists that we all have an owner or a boss and that it's either sin or God. Have you seen the lordship of sin manifest itself in your own life or in that of others? What are the names of the contemporary idols to which people give unwitting allegiance while insisting that they are free?

1 An illustration from marriage

Romans 7:1–6

Paul continues his argument and makes it clear that while he is talking to all his hearers, his primary audience is the Jewish Christians – those who know the law. Those who were born Jewish may well have understood themselves as having been born and raised under the Torah, that is, subject to its authority and rule. Today, at their bat or bar mitzvahs, Jewish young people accept the law and its obligations, and throughout history Jewish people have felt that their relationship with the law gives a particular identity. Many may not have seen themselves in Paul's previous arguments about having once been ruled by sin. Paul insists that the authority of the Torah only lasts for as long as a person lives. He compares this to being married. You are bound to your spouse until they die and after that you are free to marry again. Those who belong to Jesus have died with him and now live a new life with him. They therefore no longer belong to the law. Paul does not mean that they cease to be Jewish but that their identity is now best expressed in terms of belonging to the Messiah.

Paul argues that being under the Torah, with its focus, in part at least, on the outward, the flesh, in fact served to provoke sin – Paul will explore this in some depth in the next section – and so, whatever its intentions, the law ended up leading to death. Paul refers to the law as 'written code' and he contrasts this with the work of the Spirit of God. The code, whatever its intention, serves to stifle and control, whereas the Spirit enables people to live for God.

2 The Torah and its effects

Romans 7:7–14

Paul is aware that he could easily be misunderstood. Some might think that he is attacking the law which had been given by God. That is not his intention. He carefully distinguishes between the law and its effects. He does this by telling the story, in the first person, of the impact of the Torah. In one sense, this is Paul's own story as a Jew growing up and becoming aware of the law. In another sense, it's the story of Adam and the commandment he was given. Then again, perhaps most significantly in the original context, it's the story of Israel, the people born under the Torah. And, importantly for many readers over the centuries and today, in an extended sense, this is the story of every person who's ever experienced an inner conflict between what they know to be right and what they find themselves inclined to do. However, it's important to remember that Paul's focus is on his discussion of the Jewish law and its impact.

The Torah was God's gift to Israel and so it must be spiritual, holy, just and good. It is certainly not to be confused with sin. Nevertheless, there is a relationship between the two. Without a commandment, there can be no transgression and it is our awareness of transgressing that makes us conscious of sin. Paul illustrates this using the commandment against coveting, against desiring things that belong to others. This law puts a name to something that is almost instinctive and so makes you aware of the extent of your sinfulness. You become conscious that so much of your thinking and your longing breaks the rules. So, while the purpose of the law was to bring life, its actual result was to bring death. This was not really the fault of the law but of sin which found a foothold there that meant it could bring death to those who lived under it. It's an indication of just how perverse and dangerous sin is that it can twist to its own purposes something as good as the Torah. The law may be spiritual, but it deals with humans, in part at least, by relating to the outward dimensions of our existence, the aspect of our beings that Paul calls 'the flesh'. And this is the part of us that has a propensity to go against the purposes of God.

3 Sin leads to a conflicted Torah and a conflicted self

Romans 7:15–25

In words that resonate with every person in possession of a conscience, Paul describes the inner conflict experienced by those under the Torah – the self ends up conflicted. It can believe that the Torah is good and, inwardly, commit itself to doing what it knows is right. Nevertheless, it ends up doing the opposite because of the impact of sin on the flesh. In other words, the 'I' who acts is not the true, inner 'I' but sin, for sin is in control of the outer aspects of the 'I'. The law may tell a person to do good but, like Cain, they find sin lurking at the door (Genesis 4:7).

In other words, the 'I' under the law finds itself conflicted, pulled in different directions. And this is because the law itself is conflicted. There is an aspect of the Torah that is a delight to the inner self. Paul calls it the law of God (v. 22). However, there is another aspect of the Torah that conflicts with it. Paul calls it the law of sin and says that it has made its home in the outer parts of the 'I'. The inner person might want to obey the law of God, but their outer aspects follow the law of sin (v. 25). Small wonder the 'I' asks, echoed by many others down the centuries, 'Who will rescue me?' Paul's answer lies in God's action through Messiah Jesus. Paul claims that this helps to resolve the conflict.

4 God's answer

Paul picks up the threads of different parts of his argument and weaves them together. He refers to his discussion of wrath and judgement, and to the conclusion of chapter 6, and states that it follows from what he has said that when it comes to the final judgement, those who belong to Messiah Jesus will not be condemned. The conflict within the Torah – and within people – has been resolved because the law of the Spirit of life has freed the 'I' from the law of sin. God has done what the law could not accomplish and has done it by sending his Son as a human and dealing with sin in the place where it had made its home – human flesh. The result of this is that those who live in accordance with God's Spirit can start to live in the way God always intended, something that the law purported to achieve but could not accomplish. Those who are orientated to God's Spirit enjoy the life and peace God intended, but those who remain orientated to the flesh, to the outer aspects of human life, cannot live that way.

Paul assures his first hearers that since they have received God's Spirit, they are no longer orientated to the flesh, however they may have lived in the past. He reminds them of the power of God's Spirit which raised Jesus from the dead. They can be certain that the same Spirit will bring them life.

5 God's promises for the whole creation

Romans 8:12–27

The presence of God's Spirit in someone's life is the sign that they belong to the Messiah, and therefore that they are God's children. They have been adopted into his family so that they can call God 'Father'. Since they are God's children, they are also his heirs. We normally think of heirs as those who inherit something when someone dies. This seems awkward because we know that God cannot die. It might be better to think in terms of a trust that entitles you to receive the benefits when certain conditions are met. Through Messiah Jesus, the conditions have been met. So what Paul means by 'heirs' is those who are entitled to all the good things that God has guaranteed in his covenant promises. The true heir is of course the Messiah, but all those who belong to him are his coheirs. We see that those who are justified are the people of God, who, enabled by the Spirit, live their lives orientated towards God, and who, because they are heirs, inherit God's promises.

There is, however, a downside to all of this. Those who belong to the Messiah can expect to suffer just as he did. However, this suffering is not without meaning or purpose. Paul compares it to childbirth because it is creative. The idea is that the followers of Jesus form the vanguard of the renewed creation. The rest of creation has been waiting for them. Up to this point, creation has been enduring the decay and futility to which it was subjected when the first humans – those created by God to nurture creation and care for it – went rogue. Now humans are back on track, the rest of creation waits expectantly to be brought back in line with its own glorious original purposes.

As creation waits for the completion of this process of renewal, it too suffers. Within the suffering creation, the people of God suffer while they live in anticipation of God's next promised action. And within God's people, the Spirit of God intercedes with God as everyone involved longs for the fulness of God's promises to come to pass at the renewal of all things. Among the many wonderful things implied by this is that when we know we must pray but cannot find the words, God is at work within us with wordless prayers that express our longing for God to complete his work of putting the world back on track.

6 Cast-iron guarantees

Romans 8:28–39

Paul has argued that the whole of creation is working towards a goal and here he confirms that everything is working together towards God's greater goal for those who love God and are a part of this great purpose. Then, in a series of verbs expressed in the past but with some of them referring to things that remain future, Paul sets out one way of understanding the stages passed through by those who follow Messiah Jesus. It begins with them being fore-known and ends with them being glorified – exactly as the ancient promises would lead us to expect. And the whole process is in God's hands.

In verse 31, Paul returns to the law court imagery he used at the start of the chapter. God has already decided the case in favour of his people. There's no point in anyone turning up to read out the charge sheet. After all, Messiah Jesus has God's ear and is speaking on behalf of those who belong to him. Paul is making use of the conviction of the primitive church that Psalm 110:1 should be understood as a prophecy that was fulfilled when Jesus ascended into heaven.

Paul is defiant in the face of persecution and opposition. Though the words of Psalm 44 are being fulfilled in his own life and that of his hearers, with all the suffering that entailed, he is confident that if God has given his Son, then he can be relied upon to give everything else he has ever promised. Jesus' followers are therefore, because of what God has done, not simply those who overcome everything that may oppose them, but super- or hyper-overcomers. Nothing else in all of creation can possibly do anything to alter this. Nothing can challenge or compete with what God has done. If God has gone to such lengths to keep his promises and to demonstrate his love for his people, then there is nothing that can possibly change it. God's victory, and the victory of his people, is guaranteed.

Guidelines

The apostle has set out the conflict at the heart of human life and then shown how God has resolved it through the work of Messiah Jesus and the work of the Holy Spirit. He has celebrated the way that God has drawn people into his family so that they can inherit all his promises. Then he has gone on to show the impact that this will have on the whole of creation. Finally, Paul has insisted that since God has done this, there is nothing that can undo it. Those who belong to the Messiah are loved to the uttermost by God, and no amount of distress or suffering can change that.

- The apostle seems to argue that the command against covetousness epitomises the law or at least illustrates its impact. What made him choose this particular commandment? Is it because it might lie behind the temptation to break some of the others (theft, adultery, murder)? Or because it reflects an inward disposition rather than any necessary outward act? Or something else?

- Most of us feel conflicted at certain points in our lives. Do Paul's words in chapter 7 resonate with your own experience? How were these situations resolved?

- Paul speaks of a creation subjected to futility and anticipating being set free from its bondage. This suggests that the whole of the created world has a place in the purposes of God. Should these words affect our attitudes towards environmental issues such as climate change, pollution and the extinction of other species?

- The chapter ends with a long list of things that cannot separate God's people from God's love. Some of the categories he mentions – for example, principalities, powers, height and depth – might seem strange to contemporary ears. Can you think of ways to express these ideas in today's terms?

FURTHER READING

Matthew W. Bates, *Salvation by Allegiance Alone: Rethinking faith, works and the gospel of Jesus the king* (Baker, 2017) .

Michael F. Bird, *The Saving Righteousness of God: Studies on Paul, justification and the new perspective* (Paternoster, 2007).

Karl P. Donfried, ed., *The Romans Debate, Revised and Expanded Edition* (T & T Clark, 1991).

Paula Gooder, *Phoebe: A story* (Hodder & Stoughton, 2019).

Richard N. Longenecker, *Introducing Romans: Critical issues in Paul's most famous letter* (Eerdmans, 2011).

Richard N. Longenecker, *The New International Greek Testament Commentary: The Epistle to the Romans* (Eerdmans, 2016).

Peter Oakes, *Reading Romans in Pompeii: Paul's letter at ground level* (SPCK, 2009).

Thomas R. Schreiner, *Romans (Second Edition)* (Baker, 2018).

John R.W. Stott, *The Message of Romans* (IVP, 1994).

Anthony C. Thiselton, *Discovering Romans: Content, interpretation, reception* (Eerdmans, 2016).

A.J.M. Wedderburn, *The Reasons for Romans* (T&T Clark, 1991).

N.T. Wright, *Justification: God's plan and Paul's vision* (SPCK, 2009).

Internal twin parables

David Spriggs

Recently we explored some of the twin parables of Jesus that have been so identified by scholars. These are parables where the same or similar structure with the same or similar message can be identified. Normally these twins occur together in one or more of the gospels. By comparing these twins, we were able to consider a number of interesting issues which affect the understanding and interpretation of parables.

There is, however, another set of twin parables. Whereas the previous set could be called 'external twins', the set we consider this week are internal twins. In these, the twins appear within the same parable. For instance, at its simplest, the two sons (Matthew 21:28–31). In some ways (not least, when the context/purpose of the parable is taken into account), this parallels Luke's most famous parable that of the prodigal son – or is it really the two sons? If so, this could be considered as one of the most complex internal twins. In both of these there are not only the twins but another vital *dramatis persona*, i.e. the father. This helps to clarify what we mean by an 'internal twin'; it is not simply that there are only two characters or key subjects, but that the parable depends on a black-and-white contrast between the two key subjects in order to make its point. Indeed, this black-and-white contrast becomes an interesting issue to reflect on – which we will do in the closing 'Guidelines' section of these notes. While it is tempting to rename some of these, e.g. two temple worshippers instead of the Pharisee and the tax collector, I have kept to their more familiar names to help with recognition.

Unless otherwise stated, Bible quotations are taken from the NRSV.

1 The two housebuilders

Matthew 7:24–29; Luke 6:46–49

We start our exploration with a very familiar twin. Perhaps you first encountered it as a children's song, 'The wise man built his house upon the rock', with its repetitions and exciting climax. From the various YouTube videos, it is as popular now as 70 years ago. We do well to ask why this is so, even though the song has no context and no application, unlike the originals.

Within the gospel tradition, the context is highly significant. In Matthew and Luke, it comes at the end of a central piece of teaching by Jesus: the sermon on the mount for Matthew (chapters 5—7) and the sermon on the plain for Luke (6:20–49). In both, the same 'steer' on the meaning is given. It is about living according to the insights and directions of Jesus. For Matthew this is encapsulated in the words: 'Everyone then who hears these words of mine and acts on them will be like a wise man' (7:24); 'And everyone then who hears these words of mine and does not act on them will be like a foolish man' (6:26). And in Luke, 'I will show you what someone is like who comes to me, hears my words and acts on them' (6:47); 'But the one who hears and does not act is like a man' (6:49).

There are two points worth noting from the above. First, Luke does not categorise the men as wise and foolish. Did Luke drop these because they didn't fit his audience? Did Matthew add them because they reminded him of the Old Testament origins?

Second, Luke has a rather different start: 'Why do you call me, "Lord, Lord" and not do what I tell you?' (6:46). This introduction interrupts the style of the rest of the discourse and might indicate that it has been incorporated from elsewhere.

The parable has a number of twins: two different builders, two different houses and two different outcomes. In Matthew it even has even two different categorisations. Explaining it like this immediately reveals it is not quite as straight forward as might appear. For there are three (or four) sets of internal twins which contribute to its meaning and perhaps help to account for why it is so memorable. They act like hammer blows and drive the message into our heads.

2 The two gates/roads

Matthew 7:13–14 (compare Luke 13:22–24)

The concept of 'two ways' was familiar in the Old Testament. Psalm 1, significantly the gateway psalm, sets out two ways of life: 'Happy are those who do not follow the advice of the wicked… The wicked are not so' (Psalm 1:1, 4). Then, in its climactic verse, it claims, 'For the Lord watches over the way of the righteous but the way of the wicked will perish' (Psalm 1:6). Although this psalm is less rigorous than the parable in its presentation of the choice, in the end it is no less clear. There are two ways only: that of the righteous and that of the wicked. Their behaviours, their associations and their outcomes will be very different. Like Elijah, the challenge is: 'If the Lord is God, follow him; but if Baal, then follow him' (1 Kings 18:21).

The dichotomous presentation is not about remembering as such but about making a categorical choice and living it out. It is only in Matthew that the twins can be seen – Luke refers only to the narrow door. In Matthew there is a 'narrow gate' and a 'wide gate'; there is an 'easy road' and a 'hard road'. As in Psalm 1, the chosen routes lead to contrasting outcomes: the narrow gate and hard road lead to life; the easy road and the wide gate to destruction. However, they are not set out in the rigorous way of the two houses, in structure or language. By 'easy', we are not to think of one without ruts, boulders or steep inclines, but one that is really wide and imposing.

There is therefore debate (see Leon Morris, *The Gospel According to Matthew*, p. 175) as to whether the gates are the start of the journey or the conclusion. In the first, the gate is perceived as the start – committing ourselves to Christ (evangelical decision) and the road the daily following (ethical endurance). Those who see the gate as the point of arrival understand this as our eschatological salvation (as in *Pilgrim's Progress*). I suggest from the overall structure that the former is the intended interpretation. But the main point is that following Christ is a tough choice from beginning to end. But the one alone that is worth pursuing, as it leads to life (compare Matthew 16:24, etc. 'take up their cross').

3 The two sons

Matthew 21:28–32 (compare Luke 15:12–32)

Although there are significant textual variations for this parable which involve reversing the order of appearances and even confusing the responses, we will work from the standard NRSV text. Nevertheless, it is worth noting that these variations may indicate that this 'homely parable [which] brings out the importance of doing what is right and not merely talking about it' (Morris, p. 536), which might not be quite so straightforward and obvious as at first glance!

Matthew's gospel follows Mark very closely over the surrounding sections (compare Matthew 21 with Mark 11:1—12:12), but Matthew 'inserts' this parable between the issue of Jesus' authority and the parable of the wicked tenants, presumably because of the link with John the Baptist (Matthew 21:23–27).

The story seems straightforward enough. There are two sons of the one father. Two identical instructions, even demands, are put to the two sons, although, unlike the two housebuilders, the words are not verbalised the second time. We are only told, 'The father went to the second and said the same' (v. 30).

The response to the instruction is where the two sons part company. The first says, 'I will not'; the second says, 'I go, sir.' The first sounds surly, the second compliant and polite. But that is not the point of the parable. The point is that the first in the end goes and does what has been asked, 'to work in the vineyard'. The second, in contrast to his positive and polite verbal response, 'did not go'. But the contrast is intensified. For the first, 'later he changed his mind' (the word is the same as 'repented'), but there is no suggestion that the second changed his mind. It thus seems he not only failed to act in obedience to his father, but he also lied about his intention and was hypocritical too. While neither was the ideal son, the second's disobedience was disreputable.

But what is the application of this parable? It is not as the reference to 'the kingdom of God' would indicate, that the tax collectors and harlots are responding to Jesus, but that they had responded to John the Baptist! In other words, they recognised John's authority was from God, which the religious leaders, then as now, failed to do – they did not change their minds and believe in him. So the ultimate difference is not about obeying instructions but believing, perceiving who John and Jesus truly are.

4 The Pharisee and the tax collector

Luke 18:9–14

If the previous parable highlighted indirectly the contrast between the religious leaders and those who were considered outcasts, then this one brings them centre stage. And what a stage it is. The location is none other than the temple, the holy place, in the heart of the holy city! The stakes could hardly be higher.

It is clear we have internal twins, but there is no attempt to suggest they are similar. In the previous parable the twins are both sons of the same father, to whom the same instruction is given. Here, from very early on, it is the stark differences which are underlined. One is a Pharisee, the other a tax collector.

Why, therefore, do we consider them twins? First, they are introduced as 'two men'. For a brief moment in the story, they share the same identity; as they appear from the wings, the first thing we notice is their shared humanity. Then, not only are they heading for the same venue but they go with the same (superficial) purpose: they are going to the temple to pray. They both share a belief in Israel's God.

These tiny details, flashing by almost before the hearers had time to hear, may well have shocked them. For the audience is described as those who 'trusted in themselves that they were righteous, and regarded others with contempt' (v. 9). We may well wonder whether they could even conceive of a 'tax collector' wanting to go to the temple to pray!

The Pharisee's prayer reveals the extent of his dedication to the law and in some detail his piety (see verses 11–12 and commentaries for the details). But equally it unmistakably reveals he trusted in himself and despised others too. In contrast, we are spared the details of the tax collector's sinful activities. He simply describes himself as a sinner in need of God's mercy.

Often, Jesus asks people for their adjudication on the people in his parables or when they come to him with questions, he draws them into the answer. These are great heuristic principles. Yet here we have a pronouncement. This announcement is marked by these words, 'I tell you.' The pronouncement is in terms of contrasting twins – those who exalt themselves and those who humble themselves. It is the latter who are 'justified'.

5 Two debtors

Luke 7:40–43 (compare Matthew 18:23–35)

Here we have two parables which are both about the significance of forgiveness, and both include two parallel characters – debtors in serious trouble as they cannot pay up. But in every other respect they are different. The contexts are different and the relationship between the two characters is so too. With Luke, the two debtors are related to the one creditor; in Matthew, one debtor (who owes an enormous debt) is also the creditor of the second (who owes a relatively trivial amount). The dynamic structure and the meanings are therefore very different. These divergences perhaps encourage us to accept that Jesus could tell stories with the same components on more than one occasion and for different purposes. It takes a great leap of imagination to conclude either that Luke's is a short version of Matthew's or vice-versa. We will focus on Luke's story.

We note first that this is a story (parable) set within another story (narrative), but it lacks any kind of 'parabolic introduction' such as 'to what shall we liken it', 'he told them a parable' or 'the kingdom of heaven is like'. Second, we can identify the two characters in the parable with individuals in the narrative. Indeed, Jesus does this for us. The one who owes the most is the woman; the one whose debt is relatively trivial is Simon the Pharisee. Unusually, then, we have a male and female in the narrative pair, although not within the parable.

What is fascinating is that Jesus starts by appearing to accept the premise of the Pharisee; 'what kind of woman this is… a sinner' (7:39). Later, Jesus confirms this, 'her sins, which were many' (7:47). Intriguingly, as we superimpose the parable on the narrative like this, it emerges that the creditor must be Jesus, acting in the role of God (the only one who can forgive sins – see Luke 5:21) for in the end Jesus says to the woman, 'Your sins are forgiven.' These words are more words of assurance than pronouncement, as Jesus had already pointed out that her great expression of love shows she has already been, and experienced, God's forgiveness. In contrast, Simon's begrudging invitation to a meal, but withholding the normal courtesy of foot-washing for his honoured guest, underlines the fact that he has not experience forgiveness for his sins.

6 The ten bridesmaids

Matthew 25:1–13

Life in the villages and towns of Judea, especially for women, could be hum-drum, tedious and arduous. Fetching water, grinding corn, collecting sticks and grasses, baking, pounding clothes, spinning and weaving. The thought of a wedding, with its music and dancing, dressing up and enjoying food and wine you hadn't prepared, was certainly a high point and would generate excitement, especially among the younger ones who were the bridesmaids. This was quite a grand occasion, as there are ten of them.

They arrive at the venue and now the wait begins. Then, as now, things can go wrong at weddings. Minutes give way to hours; daylight to darkness. Their excitement wanes. Exhausted by frustrated anticipation, they all drop off to sleep. Suddenly they are roused by a shout. 'The groom is on his way, get out there to welcome him.' So, they light their lamps (or more likely torches). However, as they set off from the house, five of these bridesmaids realise they hadn't bothered about oil to keep their torches burning. They ask for a share of the others' oil, but the answer is 'No'. And while they are searching for oil, the groom arrives; the guests with the groom process into the house, led by five of the bridesmaids. Then the door is shut. For safety's sake, it must remain closed until daylight. The five who hadn't properly prepared for the long haul are locked out for good. They miss the event.

It is a clear divide – wise verses foolish – just like the housebuilders. Commentators explore which features of this story are allegorical and so might be secondary; they debate whether the coming of the bridegroom can be equated with Jesus (as the groom/husband in the Old Testament was God himself not the Messiah), and if so whether Jesus or the early church made this connection. Does it pose the challenge of Israel being ready for the arrival of the Messiah in Jerusalem (see Matthew 21:1–10) or at the end of time (see Matthew 24:29–31)?

Guidelines

As we have explored these internal twin parables, using this phenomenon is like seeing with two eyes rather than one: various nuances and insights seem to emerge and provide a richer engagement with Jesus' stories. Or to use another metaphor, reading them this way acts like shining an ultraviolet light on an old painting. Things which have been hidden by the final surface start to appear and provide us with an enhanced understanding and appreciation of the master's skills. If you have sensed this, then why not take a look at some others, such as the weeds among the wheat (Matthew 13:24–29); the sheep and the goats (Matthew 25:31–39); the good/bad tree/fruit (Matthew 7:15–20; 12:33–35; Luke 6:43–45), and see what you discover using this approach.

One of the areas we have hinted at but not investigated is what might be the source for Jesus' frequent use of internal twins. In the Old Testament, wisdom and foolishness are often polarised and, in Proverbs, even personified as two very different women (see Proverbs 7—8). In two of the parables we have looked at, this categorisation is overtly employed.

But there are other potential sources such as the righteous and the wicked (see Psalm 1:6). Further back in the Old Testament, we have the blessings and curses of Deuteronomy, for instance chapter 28. In the court you are either guilty or not guilty; in battle you either survive or die. Clearly these human experiences, with their very different outcomes, can have coloured Jesus teaching and approaches to people.

From other aspects of his teaching, we can discern his awareness of either-or situations. For instance, Matthew 24:40–41 says: 'Then two will be in the field: one will be taken and one will be left. Two women will be grinding meal together; one will be taken and one will be left.' This suggests an eschatological context for these black-and-white stories (as with the ten bridesmaids and the sheep and the goats). But others seem to presuppose an evangelical imperative – you must decide for me or against me; there is no room for dithering (see Luke 9:59–62; compare Mark 1:16–20); which gate will you enter by. Still others point towards an ethical imperative, encapsulated by the two roads, or ways of life; carrying the cross every day.

Finally, does the frequency of these internal twins, which polarise life into light and darkness, have any challenges for the style and content of our preaching? I prefer shades of grey to black and white, but did Jesus?

FURTHER READING

Kenneth E. Bailey, *Jesus Through Middle Eastern Eyes: Cultural studies in the gospels* (SPCK, 2008).

C.H. Dodd, *The Parables of the Kingdom* (Collins, 1961).

Joachim Jeremias, *The Parables of Jesus* (Scribner, 1963).

I. Howard Marshall, *The New International Greek Testament Commentary: The Gospel of Luke* (Paternoster Press, 1978).

Leon L. Morris, *The Gospel According to Matthew* (IVP, 1992).

Martyn Payne, *Messy Parables* (BRF, 2017).

Traversing time and crossing cultures

Philip Grasham

Before my wife and I moved to live and work in West Africa, we left no stone unturned in researching the history of the people group with which we would be rubbing shoulders. Similarly, we devoured everything we could lay our hands on about their culture. With all that under our belts, we arrived and began to get our tongues around new sounds and syllables. All of this was necessary to get to grips with what was to us such a strange and surprising context.

Every person is shaped and formed by the community into which they are born. This was true for Abraham, Peter, Priscilla and Anna, and it is true for each one of us as well. This means that our basic assumptions about life, our customs and our worldview are shared with those in our cultural context. Thus, what about when we delve into the scriptures and encounter people from a very different time and place?

Anthropologists and psychologists have coined the acronym WEIRD for aspects of our western culture that separate it most from the rest of the world: **W**estern, **E**ducated, **I**ndustrialised, **R**ich and **D**emocratic. Each of these five facets are a stumbling block to our knowing the ins and outs of biblical customs and values. We also need to realise that behind our English texts lie a world of images, symbols and idioms. We have just as many of these in English – I have used many English examples above to highlight this (no stone unturned, rubbing shoulders, and so on) but we do not always see these in the scriptures.

In these next few days, we will look at a selection of passages where our **WEIRD** cultural blind spots might be obscuring our understanding of the text and try to see beyond these.

Unless otherwise stated, Bible quotations are taken from the ESV.

1 Recognising context and language

Psalm 23

The shepherd metaphor runs right through the scriptures. It is associated with both the authority and affection shown by a leader – earthly or divine.

Psalm 23:1–4 outlines a typical day in the life of a shepherd as he or she guides the sheep to food and water. It is clear that without the shepherd's leading the sheep would not survive long, especially during the hot, dry season.

When we think of sheep and green pastures, we imagine creatures with thick woolly coats grazing in lush meadows. However, ancient Near Eastern sheep are smaller, with a lighter fleece. They are used to walking long distances as the shepherd leads from the front and they follow obediently behind.

As the sheep wander over the rocky terrain, they nibble on the coarse grass and weeds. It should be noted that the Hebrew makes no mention of 'green' pastures, which shows a cultural bias lacking in the original text.

Shepherds were both providers and protectors – the rod was for defence and safety; the staff was for guiding and rescuing. Although they followed their shepherd, the sheep tended to amble away. The work was demanding and dangerous, with an unbreakable bond between shepherds and their animals.

In the many wadis that can be found in the wilderness, humans and animals confront deep shadows without knowing whether there is someone or something lying in wait in the darkness. It really is walking through 'the valley of the shadow of death'.

Then the shepherd metaphor is replaced with a banquet metaphor. The connection is that setting a feast shows the care and provision of the host. In verse 5, before the guest sits down at the table, the host offers fine oils that soothe the skin and give a shine to the face. And, further still, the bounteousness of the host is seen in an overflowing and quickly replenished cup.

In verse 6, 'goodness and mercy' more vigorously 'chase' or 'pursue' (rather than merely 'follow'). Plus, the English word 'mercy' is the Hebrew word *chesed*, which is a notoriously elusive term to translate. Should it be rendered compassion, mercy, kindness, loyalty or steadfast love? The probable answer is yes, all of them and yet more as well.

May we appreciate the role of context and language as we examine the poems and stories in our Bibles.

2 Realising that the community surpasses the individual

Luke 11:1–13

Near the beginning of Luke 11, we find Jesus sharing a story about a man at midnight asking his neighbour for some bread due to the unexpected arrival of a guest. Jesus continued with a memorable statement about asking, seeking and knocking. Without digging into the text, we can miss cultural and linguistic aspects and also how these two parts are connected.

So, first, as individual Bible readers in an individualistic culture, we can fail to realise that when a guest arrives unannounced, the honour and hospitality of the village is in jeopardy even at such a late hour. The main concern of each villager is to uphold the reputation and status of their community. Consequently, every person will do whatever is necessary for this guest to be copiously cared for so that they leave with praises on their lips for the generosity and kindness of this village. This is why the door-knocking man is so confident that, while it may take a few tries, the sleepy man will eventually respond.

In Luke 11:5, the man asks for three loaves. That is one for his guest and one for himself because you do not eat alone. But why ask for three? When the guest finished his loaf, his host will offer him the third loaf to show the big-heartedness of his community. The honour code means being lavish and extravagant.

When we get to verse 9, this is a continuation of the principle of persevering in prayer. Jesus taught that we should be unceasing in asking, seeking and knocking. Jesus uses present imperatives which means that a more precise translation would be 'to ask and keep on asking… to seek and keep on seeking… to knock and keep on knocking', which connects us to the parable. The contrast is that, unlike the grumpy friend who finally helps, God is gracious, generous and enjoys giving good gifts to his children.

As we read the biblical accounts, we need to realise that each person was interdependent on the whole. Everyone needed to do their part for the good of the wider community. This meant that individual freedoms and personal rights were always secondary to what was best for others in their family and in their group.

May we comprehend the biblical emphasis on shared life where every man and woman saw themselves primarily as one who belonged to a group.

3 Recapturing a sense of the mysterious

Luke 8:22–39

In today's passage, we have Jesus rebuking the weather and exorcising demons. This is not an account of Jesus the helpful healer or even the profound preacher. What we have is something far more mysterious. As westerners, we have a propensity to doubt miracles and the activities of angels and demons. Our scientific mindset means that we often seek other explanations and discuss topography and schizophrenia for today's account. We have lost our sense of awe and wonder. Yet, there might be even darker mysteries in our text than we often realise.

In verse 23, Jesus was asleep when a thunderstorm came rolling across the lake causing the waves to surge over the sides of the boat. When the experienced fishermen began to panic, all the disciples feared for their lives. They woke Jesus and he 'rebuked' (or 'reprimanded/admonished') the storm. Jesus personally addressed the wind and the waves, using the word which was used to expel evil spirits. This tempest seems to have had a devilish origin. In relation to this, usually after a natural storm, the winds die down but the waves remain choppy for a few hours. But in verse 24 we read that there was a calm. This is an unusual term which means there was a mysterious, supernatural stillness. In Psalm 107:29 we read: 'He made the storm be still, and the waves of the sea were hushed.'

The reason for this adversarial storm seems to be that the enemy was protecting his own. Jesus safely reached the shore and was met by a demonised man who had been driven out of the city and was now living among the dead. It is here that the kingdom of God and the kingdom of Satan clash once again. Our text describes Legion as having superhuman strength, so that he was able to break chains and shackles. Nevertheless, in his awesome power, Jesus set this captive free so that he was completely liberated. The herdsmen who witnessed this miracle reported how the demon-possessed man had been healed.

While the biblical world, and much of today's world, has no issues accepting strange phenomena or activities in the unseen realm, westerners tend to be uncomfortable with things that cannot be explained and/or rationalised. May these stories not lead us to scepticism but to the worship of the storm-stiller and the demon-deliverer.

4 Reorganising the whole of our lives

Psalm 139

This is such a wonderful psalm of God's pervasive presence. We read that the Lord knows every day of our lives before we live them. As God is not restrained by time or place, he is with us in our pasts, presents and futures. We can hide from everyone else but not from God. God's knowledge of us is repeated half a dozen times in this psalm, and we should note that this 'knowing' is based on relationships. It is a personal and intimate connection. It is much more than simply having information in the mind; it involves shared personal experience. There is a heart as well as a head union. God knows us and he created us to know him in the same way – deeply and thoroughly.

In the west, we can recite this psalm without really grappling with the reality of these truths: he knows what we are thinking and what we are about to say; he knows when we go out, where we go and when we return.

It is well documented that, in the western world, we have a split perspective of what is sacred and what is secular. We have compartmentalised our lives into blocks. Consequently, we can end up believing that God is interested in us when we go to church, but he is not particularly interested in us when we go to the cinema.

The biblical understanding is that all of life is a unity and, as in our psalm today, God is ever present and involved in every aspect of our lives. We need to regard everything as spiritual rather than only the obvious things. As one preacher said, if we were to time-travel back to Capernaum and ask Jesus, 'How is your spiritual life?' the response would be, 'Huh?'

We need to follow the biblical people and hold to the sacredness of everything in life. Remember, Jesus is with us as we walk the dog, wash the dishes and wander around with our friends. Every moment can be a moment of prayer and every second the possibility exists to hear God or be nudged by the Spirit.

May we allow God to search our hearts and remind us that he is interested in us and involved with us at all times and in all places. And he wants to be much more engaged in our lives.

5 Identifying with the right people

Luke 10:25–37

We often associate ourselves with the 'heroes' in the biblical texts when we should be more honest than that and sometimes see ourselves in the 'anti-heroes'. Why, when we read the gospels, do we place ourselves among the oppressed and poor Jews, when our education and resources mean we are far more like the Herodians or the Romans looking out on an uneducated and impoverished world?

In our affluent, technologically advanced society, many of us could not be less like a poor fisherman, a disadvantaged farmer or a lowly beggar. This means we can miss some of the Messiah's piercing comments to the privileged. We should understand that God is and always has been on the side of the afflicted and the subjugated.

In today's text, we sneer at the priest and the Levite for their attitudes and behaviour rather than discern a reflection of ourselves. The *Mishnah* states that even a high priest must assure an unattended corpse receives proper burial, but the priest did not want to get involved. Similarly, the Levite does not want to get involved either. For both men, this has nothing to do with not wanting to be defiled so that they could not fulfil their duties in the temple. They are not going to Jerusalem but from Jerusalem.

Also, we can miss the fact that the first hearers were waiting for Jesus to introduce the champion in his parable, who almost certainly was going to be a Pharisee. We have vilified these men when they may be our closest likeness. One modern commentator writes that they were the evangelicals of their day. For example, Rabbi Hillel, who just predates Jesus, is the exact opposite of our usual picture of Pharisees as inflexible legalists. We so love to boo and hiss when the Pharisees appear that we fail to identify with them and see ourselves in them.

In our parable, a Pharisee would not have been shocking, but Jesus stunned his listeners by introducing a Samaritan as the star of the show. Jesus taught the value God places on human life and the lengths to which we should go to do what is just and right.

May we allow the Lord to illuminate the scriptures in such a way that we see ourselves as we truly are and we do justice and love kindness as we aid others in their poverty and suffering.

6 Responding to God in faithfulness

One problem westerners face with the biblical texts comes from a misunderstanding of the meaning of the word 'faith'. We have inherited the mindset which proposes that faith equals belief, so we are to assess and accept a series of didactic declarations as being true. This is why we have statements of faith, creeds and doctrinal affirmations. This means we concentrate on knowing what is true and making sure we hold to all the right doctrines and rules. There is obviously real value to this. However, in doing so, we have missed an important emphasis. A more biblical understanding is that faith equals faithfulness, so as God's people, we concentrate on how we should live. Our behaviour should mirror God's word as we both learn and practise what God requires of us.

In our passage, at the end of everything Jesus has taught in the sermon on the mount, including instructions on fasting, giving, loving and praying, we get to application. In verse 24, Jesus says that everyone who hears his words and puts them into action is like a wise man who built his house on a solid foundation. This involves effort and energy. The teaching of the rabbis was that we have not truly understood what we have been taught until it transforms our lives.

Conversely, the one who hears, but is not interested in the serious business of dedication and devotion, builds on a flimsy footing.

Throughout the Bible, the wise man is the one who acknowledges God and applies his truth to everyday living, while the foolish man is indifferent to instruction and casts aside correction.

Consequently, when the gale and deluge come, only one of these men will have dug down deep enough to withstand the storm.

What is interesting is that this parable is not unique to Jesus but, as he often does, he includes a surprising twist. For the Jewish teachers, the rock on which to build was the Torah or the first five books of our Old Testament. In Jesus' parable, the rock on which to build is Jesus himself. This connects with verse 29 that Jesus taught with authority.

May we recognise Jesus' authority over our lives, but may we also realise that we should practise our theology and respond to our Lord with faithfulness and obedience.

Guidelines

The cultures of the Bible are almost diametrically opposed to **WEIRD**. Therefore, we must recognise that what we know about art, architecture, economics, education, employment, medicine, politics and so on is far removed from the people and peoples we read about in the scriptures. And at a deeper level, concepts of self, ideas of family, gender roles, the importance of time, thoughts on modesty, notions of status and wealth, ideas of friendship and so on are also widely dissimilar.

Every time we pick up the Bible, we impose our ideas, feelings and values on to the text, even though we do not realise this is what we are doing. There are two things that can help us. First, we need to put in the effort to learn about biblical cultures, history and languages. There has been much that has been written with which we can engage. Second, we need to expose ourselves to the writings of non-western scholars and theologians. The authors of the so-called global south are extremely useful in showing us things we have never seen before. As we consult as wide a range as possible of scholars – men and women – from Africa, Asia and South America, as well as those from western nations, we will begin to appreciate and perceive the scriptures in their vibrant, profound fullness.

Questions for reflection

- What struck you the most in these readings? What aspect are you most interested in finding out about more?
- Why do you think studying the scriptures from a cultural-historical perspective is important and what difference will this make to your ministry?
- Search online for da Vinci's, *The Last Supper*. Now, thinking culturally, how many differences do you think there are between this 15th-century Italian painting and the real first-century Jewish last supper?

FURTHER READING

Marvin J. Newell, *Crossing Cultures in Scripture: Biblical principles for mission practice* (IVP, 2016).

Katie J. Rawson, *Crossing Cultures with Jesus: Sharing good news with sensitivity and grace* (IVP, 2015).

Lois Tverberg, *Reading the Bible with Rabbi Jesus: How a Jewish perspective can transform your understanding* (Baker Books, 2018).

Marvin R. Wilson, *Our Father Abraham: Jewish roots of the Christian faith* (Eerdmans, 1989).

N.T. Wright and Michael F. Bird, *The New Testament in its World: An introduction to the history, literature, and theology of the first Christians* (SPCK, 2019).

Jonah, Haggai, Nahum and Habakkuk

Pauline Hoggarth

A prayer from the second century BC suggests a unifying theme for those books we know as the minor prophets: 'May the bones of the Twelve Prophets send forth new life from where they lie, for they comforted the people of Jacob and delivered them with confident hope' (Han and Coggins, p. 4). The four books we read over the next weeks are not presented in their biblical or chronological order, but as their chapters best fit six weekly readings. Some scholars identify a complementarity between the earlier collection of the first six prophecies (Hosea to Micah) and the second six (Nahum to Malachi) dating to late pre-exilic and post-exilic times. They also suggest that human wrongdoing is the primary theme in the first group and resolution of wrongdoing the keynote of the second group.

All true prophets are characterised by a dual alertness – an attentiveness to their world and to the word of God. Each of the prophets we meet over the next weeks is deeply conscious of what is happening in the life of his community and the surrounding nations and is listening for God's word to his people (and, in the case of Jonah, initially deliberately deaf to it). The story of Jonah and the oracles of Haggai, Nahum and Habakkuk engage our imagination at many levels, not least (with the exception of Jonah) in their rich poetry. They offered God's people an alternative vision, an invitation to change direction, to live differently, to be transformed. As we reflect on these ancient words in openness to God's Spirit, we are also called to look, pray and work for God's newness in our lives, societies and faith communities.

Unless otherwise stated, Bible quotations are from the NRSV. Author references are to works in the 'Further reading' list.

1 Running away from God

Jonah 1

This text is quite different from what we usually think of as prophecy. Jonah is unique among the twelve minor prophets. Instead of God's oracles to his people through his spokesman, we find a story about a man who is never described as a prophet and who actually rebels against his prophetic task. The task itself is also different: Jonah is sent, not to alert or encourage his own people, but to warn the bandit kingdom of Assyria and specifically its capital, Nineveh, that God has his eye on their wickedness. Instead of the poetry characteristic of other prophets, this book is, with one brief exception (2:2–9), a prose narrative, a satirical didactic story. Jonah's sparse biography (v. 1) is slightly expanded in the history of Israel's kings (2 Kings 14:23–27). This son of Amittai came from the northern town of Gath-hepher near Nazareth and preached during the long reign of Jeroboam II in Samaria (786–746BC). But these brief historical details do not mean the story should be read as anything other than a powerful and surprising parable that seeks a response.

Jonah's drastic disobedience would not have shocked those who originally heard the story. As we shall see in the book of Nahum, Nineveh symbolised all the cruelty and violence of Assyria which Israel had experienced. As Jonah eventually explains (4:2), he wanted nothing to do with serving a merciful God who was likely to give Nineveh a chance – and maybe (some commentators suggest) jeopardise his reputation as a prophet. Jonah heads for the port of Joppa near modern Tel Aviv and finds a ship sailing west – Tarshish was probably a Spanish port – 'away from the presence of the Lord' (v. 3).

The focus of this opening chapter is on the behaviour of Jonah and the men manning his ship. The responses of the ship's crew provide a moving and thought-provoking contrast to Jonah's escapism and passivity, his attempt at oblivion (v. 5). In the eye of the storm, the multicultural mariners pray to their gods and take action to save lives. These are spiritually aware and humane men, refusing to sacrifice Jonah even when they understand his guilt, responsive to God's merciful power (vv. 15–16). Like the people of Nineveh, they represent the outsiders, while Jonah represents the insiders, the people of God. 'This story is a word to insiders concerning outsiders… a word addressed to the people of God concerning the people of the world' (Limburg, p. 144).

2 Prayer from a dark place

The anonymous author of this story (not necessarily Jonah himself) makes use of a range of literary devices to reinforce his message. One of these is the recurrent use of the word 'down': Jonah's flight from God has taken him steadily downwards, down to Joppa, down into the ship's hold and now for what seems the final act, down into the realm of death (1:3, 5; 2:5–6) where he experiences God's extraordinary rescue and responds to it in prayer.

The prayer of distress and thanksgiving attributed to Jonah is made up of selections from other psalms of praise (at least eight psalms are quoted). It includes four standard elements: a summary of answered prayer, a description of personal crisis and God's response and a vow of continuing worship. There is nothing standard though about the author's intention in placing the psalm immediately after his vivid description of the pagan sailors' prayers. He wants this deliberate juxtaposition to confront his listeners or readers with the implications of the final urgent prayer of these 'outsiders', not now addressed to their various deities but to Jonah's God (1:14), as well as the implications of Jonah's similar but belated cry for help: 'He who failed to pray, leaving it to the pagan sailors, eventually catches up with their spirit of supplication and submission' (Allen, p. 219). It seems that God listens and responds equally to open-minded pagans and rebellious prophet.

Jonah's prayer from the depths closes on a note of rededication and heartfelt praise – and perhaps a hint of what he has learned from watching and listening to the ship's crew and of being on the receiving end of their actions. Their panic-stricken prayers had been directed at first 'each… to his god' but finally to the Lord whom even the winds and waves obey (1:14–16). Did the sailors' reorientation and recognition of God's sovereignty remind Jonah of the true loyalty which he had so drastically forsaken?

At this point the dramatic tensions of the story remain unresolved: will Jonah obey God? Will Nineveh be destroyed? Maybe most importantly, to what extent is the spewed-up prophet a different person? To what extent has his worldview changed?

3 God of the second chance

Unfamiliarity with scripture may be an advantage! It makes it more likely that the Bible will take us by surprise because we don't know what happens next. The story of Jonah, like the story of Noah and his ark, may have become domesticated for us, tamed, reduced to a strange tale of a man swallowed by a huge fish. It's crucial to read the story of Jonah with a strong sense that the prophet had no script in front of him, no stage directions and no inside information about what would happen next. He has already improvised his part in God's story by drastic disobedience. Now, reoriented by God's rescue of him and by the surprising improvisations of those sailor 'outsiders', Jonah improvises quite differently, responding with unquestioning obedience to God's patiently repeated directions. Like Peter after his denial of Jesus, Jonah is experiencing the kindness of the God of second chances.

Like Jonah, the city of Nineveh also experienced the kindness of this God, determined to give the people another opportunity to respond to his word, to change and to escape destruction.

Commentators debate whether the description of the vast metropolis is a case of artistic exaggeration, an aspect of the satirical nature of the story, or really reflects the reality of Sennacherib's (the king of Nineveh) ambitious building programme. The writer certainly wants his audience to enter into the hopelessness of the situation – to imagine the solitary prophet setting out to proclaim an unwelcome, indeed unreasonable, message to a vast population.

Once more, the narrative takes us by surprise in its account of the reactions to Jonah's message of more 'outsiders' – the citizens of Nineveh and its king. We should surely expect rejection and mockery of such an unsophisticated message. Instead, these Assyrian outsiders behave like repentant insiders, with belief, fasting and symbolic actions of grief. Even more astonishingly, repentance and changed behaviour go right to the top. The parallels between the king's behaviour and that of the ship's captain in chapter 1 are striking – compare the tentative humility of the captain in 1:6 and the king in 3:9. Both recognise the final arbitration of a higher power.

The parallels between the narratives of chapter 1 and chapter 3 make the audience expect a happy ending – a Jonah delighted to witness the mercy of the God who had rescued him from the storm now repeated in mercy to the city. But Jonah's improvisation takes him in a shocking new direction.

4 What makes us angry?

The story of Jonah, like the parable Jesus told centuries later about the lost son, his brother and their forgiving father, is the story of God's scandalous grace, his outrageous determination to reach out to all the world with the good news of his love and forgiveness. As Jonah began to understand how the script had changed (3:10), he would surely have found common ground with the older brother in Jesus' story. Both are characterised by their furious rejection of an unconditional love that refuses to measure out mercy to match virtuous behaviour (Luke 15:28). Jonah rejects the service of a God who changes his mind about punishment. Jonah would rather die than serve the purposes of grace.

The closing chapter of the story is skilfully constructed to deliver its message with maximum effect. Jonah's speech and God's response deliberately balance each other, each with 39 Hebrew words. Jonah doesn't move beyond an orthodox statement of what he believes about God – a statement that is fundamentally about the Lord's relationship with his covenant people Israel (v. 2); he apparently has no understanding of God's grace extended to all peoples. The Lord's gentle, probing question, 'Is it right for you to be angry?', leaves Jonah untouched, as he sulkily withdraws to watch what will happen to the city.

But it's not only to the metropolis of Nineveh that God offers his patient mercy; it's also to his furious, bigoted messenger. The Lord enables Jonah actually to experience physically how both grace and judgement feel – like the refreshing, life-saving shade of cool green leaves on a sweltering day followed next morning by the destruction of all shelter and no escape from the deadly heat.

For one last time, God's question probes Jonah's angry reaction to the destruction of his sheltering plant and draws a stark contrast with his indifference to the fate of the human and animal inhabitants of Nineveh. The word translated 'concerned' in verses 10 and 11 is better expressed as 'to pity' and implies to weep over – God weeps over the great city, its helpless people and its non-human inhabitants.

This strange and unsettling story remains unresolved. Jonah is silent. Like Jesus' story of the lost son and his brother, it confronts the original hearers and ourselves with the question of where we find ourselves in the narrative.

5 Time to build

God's word, communicated to the people of Judah by the prophet Haggai, could not be more specific in terms of timing and circumstances. In 538BC the Persian king Cyrus had allowed some 50,000 Jews and their servants, exiled in Babylon, to return to Jerusalem with a mandate to rebuild the temple, wrecked by the Babylonians in 587BC. The opening chapters of Ezra narrate the enthusiastic start of the project and how after a couple of years it ground to a halt in the face of local hostility. Only the foundations were in place when Cyrus was replaced by Darius as king. He decided to act on the rediscovered edict of Cyrus and approved continued work on the temple. Ezra's narrative makes clear that the prophets Haggai and Zechariah were instrumental in the process (Ezra 5:1–2; 6:14).

The record of Haggai's prophecies has been carefully edited into five sections, chronologically dated to five periods in the year 520BC, the second year of Darius' reign. The main obstacle the prophet faces in the first month is not a need for official permission for temple restoration – that has been granted. It is his people's inertia and their misdirected priorities: 'Is it a time for you yourselves to live in your panelled houses, while this house lies in ruins?' (v. 4). In unhesitating response, Haggai claims that God's message is that the people should 'bring wood and build the house' (v. 8).

Haggai's single-minded focus on the restoration of the temple may raise questions for us. Scholars point out that previous Israelite prophets had questioned the building of a temple, condemned the hypocritical worship that often went on there and forecast its destruction. In refocusing his people's efforts on the temple, Haggai apparently contradicts what God has said before. 'No cry for social justice… no assurance that God dwells with the humble and contrite. Instead, he reeks of… the external and superficial religion of which we would all like to be rid' is one commentator's provocative evaluation (Achtemeier, p. 95).

Haggai's repeated prophetic challenge to 'consider how you have fared' (vv. 5, 7) alerts us to how the Lord views the situation in Judah and Jerusalem and how he wants his people to begin to see it. Only the elite enjoy that luxury housing. For most of the population life is a daily struggle to survive, to get by. And this impoverished half-life is the outcome of forgetting God, of a fruitless obsession with comfort and prosperity.

6 Take courage

As well as being open to God's Spirit and receptive to his word, Haggai had to respond to the deeply emotional reactions of his fellow Jews as they remembered how things used to be – the glory of Solomon's temple as it had been nearly 70 years before. With the wisdom and compassion of the Spirit, Haggai encourages this remembering, inviting his community and its leaders Zerubbabel and Joshua to stand in the 'nothingness' of the temple ruins, barely touched yet by reconstruction, to recall past glory but, above all, to look forward and 'take courage'. Ezra 3:10–13 tells us it was a day of mixed emotions, of deep joy and grief.

In this charged atmosphere, Haggai articulates a vision of the newness that the Lord will bring about, a newness rooted in his unchanging covenant (v. 5) and promising a glorious future – nothing less than God's kingdom on earth, the kingdom that cannot be shaken, as the writer to the Hebrews understood when he quoted Haggai (Hebrews 12:26). This power of God to generate newness invites his people – invites us – to join his work, their weakness to his strength, to take courage, to refuse to fear and to trust God's living presence among them, among us.

The closing section of Haggai takes us by surprise after the joyful promises of verse 9. Some nine weeks into the temple reconstruction, God prompts his prophet to tell a warning parable, a brief story about what makes people holy, clean in the eyes of God. Maybe there was talk going around about involvement in the temple building somehow improving people's standing with God, making them more holy. The examples the priests are asked to comment on (vv. 12–13) make clear that sinfulness and impurity contaminate everything (v. 14). It seems there is no solution for the people's carelessness about God's standards. God's warnings have touched every aspect of life, but there has been no responsive obedience (vv. 16–17).

Nevertheless, God's promise of newness still stands. The closing movements of Haggai's prophecy are dated to December and the start of the rainy season when farmers would be looking out for signs of germination and growth – the promise of blessing and of a cosmic tsunami as God moved his people towards her true destiny (vv. 21–23).

Guidelines

- To what extent have the readings in Jonah been surprising or even shocking for you? 'A Jonah lurks in every Christian heart, whimpering his insidious message of smug prejudice, empty traditionalism and exclusive solidarity' (Allen, p. 235).

- Why is it apparently such a struggle to trust in the grace of God towards ourselves and towards others? Why does adherence to the 'law' feel safer? What kind of experiences can reorientate us towards grace?

- 'The ultimate danger of temple building, and indeed of all works of religion, is the temptation to become self-righteous: to believe that association with the things of God automatically communicates... those qualities associated with holiness' (Achtemeier, p. 102). The Covid pandemic forced congregations to rethink patterns of worship, with less emphasis on meeting in church buildings. To what extent has this been a positive development? How does Haggai's call to his people to rebuild the temple feed into these discussions?

1 Is this our God?

Nahum 1

On the river Tigris in Iraq, about 400 kilometres north of Baghdad, the city of Mosul is the capital of Nineveh province. Across the river from the modern city (badly damaged in the conflicts of 2014–17) lie the ruins of ancient Nineveh, the Assyrian capital, destroyed in 612BC by a coalition of Babylonians and Medes. Nahum's prophecy emerged some time after 663BC when Thebes fell (3:8); it looks ahead to the destruction of Nineveh and the decline of the Assyrian empire which had caused such devastation both in the northern kingdom of Israel and in Judah (see, for example, 2 Kings 18:9–15).

We know very little about Nahum; some traditions locate his hometown of Elkosh (v. 1) in Judah and connect him to the tribe of Simeon. His name means 'comfort' or 'comforter' – the same word that opens the second part of Isaiah (40:1), who years earlier also confronted Assyrian power (2 Kings 19).

Nahum's prophecy is a biblical Cinderella, excluded from the church's lectionaries and rejected by many commentators as narrowly nationalistic and vengeful, though they may acknowledge Nahum's skill as a poet. The opening hymn or poem of chapter 1:2–11 provides the theological underpinning for Nahum's message, but it is also the section that is most often selectively read, quoted or avoided. The God that Nahum worships doesn't turn a blind eye to the cruelties and corruption of the Assyrian empire; he will 'by no means clear the guilty' (v. 3). But his retribution will not be carelessly impetuous. This 'good' God (v. 7) is 'slow to anger', as Judah knew well – they had suffered the horrors of Assyrian expansion and occupation for over a century. The Hebrew poetry of verses 2–11 is in the form of an acrostic that reinforces this sense of outrage under control.

We can tend to think of two Gods, the wrathful God of the Old Testament and the New Testament's God of grace and mercy. But Nahum's understanding of the God who deals with evil and wrongdoing is also a New Testament theme. Paul calls followers of Jesus to reject personal revenge and 'leave room for the wrath of God' (Romans 12:19). In the closing section of chapter 1 (vv. 12–15), Nahum moves to the implications for his people of trusting in this God of judgement and mercy – the promise that God will finally cut off the power of evil incarnate (v. 15, 'the wicked').

2 'I am against you'

The second chapter of Nahum takes the form of an oracle of judgement, a prophetic vision of the Babylonian coalition's imminent attack on the outskirts of Nineveh and its inhabitants (vv. 3–4) – horses, chariots and warriors, the cacophony of battle, uniforms of foe and friend (the Assyrians wore blue, the Babylonians scarlet – v. 3, Ezekiel 23:5–6, 14), the chaos and terror of all-out war. By verse 5 the conflict has moved to the city walls – a 'mantelet' (v. 5) was a kind of weapon-proof shelter against the hail of arrows and other missiles. But resistance comes too late, the walls have been breached and the defenders flee in panic (v. 8). Various traditions associate the downfall of Nineveh with water, but it is unclear if this was because of enemy action redirecting the water courses or the seasonal flooding of the Khusar stream that flowed through the city (vv. 6–8). The supposedly impregnable fortress of Nineveh lies exposed and vulnerable, her wealth for the taking.

Nahum's poetry now takes to ironic taunts that mock the arrogant lion that symbolised Assyrian power in statues and sculptures (vv. 11–13). The hopeful promise to 'cut off' Judah's enemy forever (1:15) echoes again in the direct threat to 'cut off' the prey of the Assyrian lion (2:13). The voices of Assyrian messengers making ever-increasing demands (v. 13) will be silenced, replaced by the voice that proclaims the good news of peace (1:15).

What brings about this reverse? 'See, I am against you, says the Lord of hosts' (v. 13 and 3:5). 'How we as nations and individuals stand in the eyes of God finally determines our death or life… Faith… needs always to ask if it deserves these words that God addressed to Assyria, "See, I am against you"' (Achtemeier 1986, p. 22).

3 Mortally wounded

As we reflect on this disturbing text, it is important to remember that a canonical reading of Nahum in scripture, specifically as one of the twelve minor prophets, locates his words alongside another account of anger on which we reflected last week – not now directed against Nineveh, but against the God who is passionately determined on mercy for the helpless people of that city (Jonah 4:1–2, 11).

Three 'oracles of woe' bring Nahum's prophecy to a close (vv. 1–7, 8–13, 14–19). This was a recognised Hebrew poetic form that made an accusation and then described the resulting punishment. It is the unswerving nature of God's faithfulness to his people, and his loathing of the careless fickleness that so often seduced them, that prompt the ugly images of verses 4–5. God abhorred Nineveh's long history of violent conquest, greed and corruption (vv. 1–4) and now announces the judgement to come (vv. 4–7). Women readers of scripture often struggle with what seems to be a depressing Old Testament tendency to equate unfaithfulness and weakness (vv. 4, 13) with female behaviour. But the imagery is not uniformly gender-specific; in several Old Testament texts God's faithfulness is powerfully communicated in terms of feminine characteristics (see, for example, Isaiah 66:13; Hosea 13:8). How could this not be when maleness and femaleness are both fully realised in God himself (Genesis 1:27)?

The second oracle (vv. 8–13) boldly taunts Nineveh with memories of Thebes, the Egyptian capital sacked by the Assyrians in 663BC. For all her defences and her allies Thebes fell, and, warns Nahum, 'You also…' (v. 11). There is no hiding place from God's righteous anger.

Nahum's closing oracle first taunts the Assyrians, urging them with heavy irony to make pointless preparations for a siege (vv. 14–17). The taunts turn into a closing funeral dirge as Nahum turns his spotlight on the Assyrian leadership – the king and those who share power (vv. 18–19). Notice the criteria by which God judges political leaders and the behaviour for which he condemns them.

4 'O Lord, how long...?'

All the information available to us about the prophet Habakkuk is internal to the prophecy itself and conclusions we may draw from it. For example, the musical directions scattered through chapter 3 (3:1, 9, 13, etc.) may suggest that Habakkuk was a worship leader in the Jerusalem temple, perhaps a Levite. His book is a dialogue with God – Habakkuk's prayers of intercession for his people and the Lord's responses during the period of the Babylonians' (Chaldeans', v. 6) rise to power against the Assyrians and the fall of Nineveh in 612BC. In 597BC Jerusalem fell to the Chaldeans and was destroyed in 587BC and its people scattered. Habakkuk's times were marked by violence, conflict and injustice.

Against this background the prophet grievingly surveys the state of his community. His opening lament (vv. 2–4) focuses on how his people have abandoned and distorted God's laws for a just and peaceable society. The systems for maintaining healthy order among people have failed – and an apparently impassive God is, for now, silent. There is a deep weariness about this prayer which we may well identify with as we pray today for our world and for more personal situations.

God's response is no easy word of comfort (vv. 5–11). It must have shocked and confused Habakkuk and his community. God has in fact *not* gone off duty; he is active – but in the most disturbing ways: 'I am rousing the Chaldeans... their own might is their god!' God's justice, ignored and distorted by his people, is to be replaced by the 'justice' of Babylon (v. 7), characterised as violent, greedy and merciless. 'Such a word from God implies that the turmoil and violence and death in our societies may not be evidence of God's absence from our lives but instead the witness to his actual working in judgment as he pursues his purpose' (Achtemeier, p. 38).

This is the response of the prophet as, in the company of Jeremiah and Ezekiel, he acknowledges that God will allow Babylon to judge his unfaithful people (v. 12b). By faith he believes they will not be utterly destroyed (v. 12a) but he nevertheless struggles with the prophetic vision of his corrupt society replaced, by God's will, with an entirely godless one: 'when the wicked swallow those more righteous than they' (v. 13). It seems as if there is no shape or purpose in human life (v. 14) and no end in sight to human destruction and suffering (vv. 15–17).

5 Keep watch, wait…

The opening section of chapter 2 gives us a strong sense of the relationship of Habakkuk with his God. In the face of the Lord's mysterious and puzzling purposes, Habakkuk determines to stand resolute, keep watch and wait in expectation that his trustworthy God will, in his own time, respond to his prophet's agonising questions. Scripture speaks often of the discipline of hopeful waiting and listening for God's word to us, a hard discipline to learn in our culture of instant information. How long did Habakkuk have to wait, listening and watching alertly for God's intentions? How soon did it become clear to him that the Babylonian invasion actually *was* part of God's plans; the timetable had not failed (v. 3). The thoughtful stance of the faithfully waiting prophet contrasts sharply with the precarious arrogance of Babylon whose security depended on the wealth of violent conquest (v. 5).

'Alas for you' – the litany of woes that follows makes clear that the idols that control human value systems are unchanged since Habakkuk's times. The vision of Babylon's greed and violence (vv. 3–5) broadens out in the rest of the chapter into a general lament about human power, wealth and pride – and their futility. The details may remind us of recent headlines: the underpinning global issue of inequality, often related to crippling debt and taxation (vv. 6–7); 'you have plundered many nations' through the slave trade and oppressive colonial regimes (v. 8); and the details of verse 17 highlight the relationship of human beings and the created world, so often destructive and exploitative. Throughout these accusations tolls the note of warning – winners may suddenly become losers: 'then you will be booty for them', 'the violence done to Lebanon will overwhelm you' (vv. 7, 17). There is no peaceful stability for those who live by violence and greed, those who have trusted false gods (vv. 18–20).

We must read these warnings 'over against ourselves', as Dietrich Bonhoeffer urged, not pointing the finger at others. They are a call to repentance, to a redirected life, to an examination of our own values, on a personal level and in relation to our society, even our church community. Habakkuk lived, as we do, with the tensions of *hearing* God's commitment to do justice and the promise of his shalom (v. 14), but *witnessing* the seeming success of the unjust and arrogant. It's often a struggle to wait in awe-stricken silence (v. 20).

6 I stand in awe

We can only guess at Habakkuk's experience of God that brought about the awed outpouring of praise that closes his prophecy. Maybe his willingness to be patiently silent in his struggling with the Lord made it possible for him to see things differently. The imminent action of God in judgement against the oppressors stirs deep horror in him (v. 16); he pleads for mercy even for them (v. 2b).

Between these two autobiographical glimpses is a hymn-vision (vv. 3–16), complete with musical directions ('Shigionoth' in verse 1 may be related to a word for lament and 'Selah' may indicate a pause in the singing or a response meaning 'forever'). God reveals himself to his prophet in an overwhelmingly powerful sound-and-vision theophany in response to Habakkuk's humble recognition of the issues that matter – not his role and reputation in this crisis situation but God's work in the world (v. 2). Like Moses gazing out over the promised land or the disciples present at Jesus' transfiguration, Habakkuk experiences a magnificent long view of God's purposes, of that last battle that will finally defeat the power of evil and rescue the trusting and suffering poor (v. 14).

The disturbing nature of the vision leaves Habakkuk weak and shaken (v. 16). Nothing has changed in terms of the conflict between good and evil in his immediate world. The Babylonian armies still threaten. And yet *everything* has changed through the vision he has had of God's purposes: 'You came forth to save your people, to save your anointed' (v. 13). As he waits to see how God will turn the tide, Habakkuk pours out his heart in a most beautiful song of trust and praise (vv. 17–19). The circumstances of the prophet's trust are almost certainly the immediate ones of Babylonian invasion and the resulting destruction of crops and livestock: 'Habakkuk is setting forth the faith that knows how to live "in the meantime" (2:4)' (Achtemeier p. 59).

The prophet's confidence in God asks questions of our faith; as I write, conflict drags on in eastern Europe, bombs fall in Yemen, conflict and famine cause increasing numbers of refugees, poverty and hunger are daily realities in the UK. How can we be trusting without being triumphalistic? Can we be trusting without being actively involved in the work of God's kingdom?

Guidelines

When we experience despair in the face of the world's injustices and oppression, Nahum provides us with words to intercede with rightful indignation on behalf of those who suffer violence and disaster.

- What causes God to say to a nation, 'I am against you' (Nahum 2:13)? Habakkuk made two assumptions about God which are likely to be true of us as Christians. He believed that God was at work and active in history and that he was utterly holy and good. Both of these foundational beliefs were tested to the limit as the prophet witnessed the success of evil, the perversion of justice and the involvement of an alien and wicked power as God's means of judgement.
- What are the current conflicts and situations around the globe which test our trust in God's sovereignty and utter reliability?

A prayer for trust in God:

O Lord, whose way is perfect, help us always to trust in your goodness, that walking with you and following you in all simplicity, we may possess quiet and contented minds, and may cast all our care on you, for you care for us; for the sake of Jesus Christ our Lord.

Christina G. Rossetti, 1830, adapted

FURTHER READING

Elizabeth Achtemeier, *Nahum–Malachi, Interpretation: A Bible commentary for teaching and preaching* (John Knox Press, 1986).

Leslie C. Allen, *The New International Commentary on the Old Testament: The Books of Joel, Obadiah, Jonah and Micah* (Eerdmans, 1976).

Richard Coggin and Jin H. Han, *Six Minor Prophets Through the Centuries* (Wiley-Blackwell, 2011).

James Limburg, *Hosea–Micah, Interpretation* (John Knox Press, 1988).

Dan Schmidt, *Unexpected Wisdom: Major insight from the minor prophets* (Baker Books, 2002).

J. Goldingay and P. Scalise, *New International Biblical Commentary: Minor Prophets II* (Hendrickson, 2009).

A 'Christian' form of lament

Tim Judson

For many around the world, Covid-19 brought the reality of suffering to the foreground of our lives. Struggles with mental health, social isolation and genuine fear of physical suffering in multiple ways have understandably prompted many of us in the church to consider the language and posture of lament. However, this does highlight something important for many of us in the relatively sanitised safety of the western world. The sobering and profound reality is that, for some people, lament is the normal expression of their life experience. Some of us are momentarily stopped when we experience forms of acute suffering. But for others, life involves the struggle of constant suffering, embodied in numerous ways. Lament provides a faithful language and response for believers in the midst of this.

For lament, we often (quite rightly) turn to places such as the books of Psalms, Job, Lamentations or Jeremiah. These portions of the Hebrew scriptures immerse us in a biblical imagination that necessarily disrupts many of us, and comforts others. However, we sadly may overlook the places in the New Testament where the church bears sorrow, sin and suffering through lament. In the following reflections, we will explore together what it means to lament as the body of Christ, as those who hope in the resurrection, who believe Jesus has defeated all sin and who rejoice in the midst of suffering, but in a way that is truly Christlike, truly human, truly faithful. We need to relearn the way of lament in the western church today. The Christian community is a body of people in the world reconciled to God through Christ. Christ's own lament is embodied in the church, for and with the world that is bound to God through his suffering love.

Unless otherwise stated, Bible quotations are taken from the NRSV.

1 Lament as faithfulness

Matthew 26:36–46

When Jesus was faced with the unspeakable horror that awaited him on the cross, he bore it through prayer in the garden of Gethsemane. It seems as though his life was at times painful, but on this occasion, it was agonising and unbearable. He didn't 'man up' or retain a 'stiff upper lip', but nor did he turn inwards in passive despair and resignation. Some people have no idea how deep and dark the evil in this world can be. Here, Jesus is reckoning with it all in his body, which includes his mind. Maybe he is beginning to spiral into an abyss, and so he pleads with his closest friends, 'I am deeply grieved, even to death; remain here, and stay awake with me' (v. 39). Then he turns to his Father in prayer. 'My Father, if it is possible, let this cup pass from me; yet not what I want but what you want' (v. 39).

He longs for comfort, for some sense that everything will be alright. He checks and discovers that his friends have fallen asleep, leaving him to bear all this in isolation. He prays again. Maybe he knows that there will be no resolution for his prayer, no positive mental attitude to muster in himself and hide behind. This is not going to go well; that's the heart of being human sometimes. The answer Jesus gets to his prayer is a non-answer. He is going to die. He is going to experience the ultimate death, separation from God, from others and from the world.

None of us can fully identify with what Jesus has suffered for us. However, we look at Gethsemane and we encounter the God who has descended into the deepest darkness, so that none of us will ever be alone in ours. When we are overcome with sorrow, enslaved to thoughts or experiences which debilitate us, Christ is there. We might not 'feel' him close by. We may not be able to rationally 'know' that he is there. Sometimes it is all beyond us. But that was the same for Jesus. He experienced that too – prayer without answers, no comfort or renewed zeal – just utter bleakness. And the reality here is that Jesus is with us regardless of what we feel or know, because God has borne our sense of abandonment for us.

2 Lament as reality

Matthew 2:13–18

Have you ever heard someone preach an Advent sermon on the not-so-nice parts of the nativity? If you have, you are in the minority. What on earth was Matthew thinking when he decided to put this into our Christmas story?

When I was a kid, Christmas was obviously the most important time of the year. For me, Jesus was cool, but Santa was even better! As the years have gone by, I have grown to treasure the Advent season as an opportunity to contemplate the mystery and outrageous wonder of the incarnation. I must admit, I now enjoy the excitement of Santa with my own kids as well. But Christmas is not exclusively fun for all people. Within all the hype, busyness and celebration, Christmas can be pretty tough. It can spark traumatic or painful memories for some people, and for others, it highlights all the more how lonely they feel.

In our church, we have a special Advent service called 'Blue Christmas'. It's not an original idea, but it's a simple service designed to create a safe space for those who are 'blue' at Christmas time. For me, it's undoubtedly the most worthwhile part of Advent. It feels more real than the glitter and the parties and the cute nativity play. It might sound a bit Scrooge-like to some, but it's actually wonderfully hopeful. People feel acknowledged. They feel known, and ultimately, they feel loved, because we have welcomed them where they are at, with the claim that God is with them too.

The scriptures remind us that even Christmas should recognise sorrow alongside joy. When God took on flesh in the world, there was a barbaric slaughter of innocent children. I don't want to bring us down for the sake of it. Rather, I want to emphasise that the gospel is good news for the poor, for the hurting, for those who are crushed and then ignored. Let's not resist God in the world. Let's not evade God's story in the cries of others. As the church, the hands and feet of Jesus himself, we are called to hear and to comfort those who hurt. After all, we rejoice with those who rejoice and mourn with those who mourn (Romans 12:15). We share in Christ's fullness of life, bound to him and, therefore, bound to the world for which he has come.

3 Lament as protest

Since Jesus ascended to heaven, the Holy Spirit has come in power and filled the disciples with the courage and necessary gifts to proclaim the gospel, this radical news which is for both Jews and Gentiles. The church is booming, and God's people are flying by the seat of their pants in trying to keep up with the Holy Spirit's lead. Numerous challenges present themselves, not least in the form of political and religious opposition (a devastating combination). Here at the end of Acts 7, the first member of Christ's body is murdered.

Stephen was a devout man, full of faith, grace and the power of the Holy Spirit (6:5, 8). He performed great signs and wonders among the people, and also took responsibility for the marginalised in the church. This guy was no flaky believer; he was hardcore! But despite his faithfulness, no, precisely because of his faithfulness, he gets martyred. In the midst of prayers for forgiveness over his enemies, the haters close their ears, gnash their teeth and silence God's man (7:54–60).

Stephen, God's child, is stoned to death. We have no time or space to pause, because that same day, the church becomes severely persecuted in Jerusalem, and everyone except the apostles is scattered. Furthermore, the zealous Pharisee, Saul, is in hot pursuit, ravaging the church house by house, imprisoning or killing more as he goes. But do you notice? In the midst of this, a few people stop. In response to the calamity and chaos of this event, Acts 8:2 says that 'devout men buried Stephen and made loud lamentation over him'.

Currently, when life is so uncertain and unprecedented, we should pause for lament. At a time when the church is still new and fresh, it finds itself beating its chest and crying out over the intrusion of death into this new life. Even here, in these early chapters of Pentecost power, suffering and tears are a feature of the church. More than that, mourning and the interruption of grief are a stark witness to Christ's protest against death, sin and evil.

4 Lament as blessing

Being a disciple of Jesus is complex. He promises to be with us, but his presence does not prevent suffering. In fact, sometimes, following Jesus can involve more suffering. I'm not talking here about getting ill or encountering difficulties within the finitude and limits of our humanness. Those things can be very painful, but they are not necessarily a form of suffering that is caused by being a Christian.

With Jesus, as the New Testament witnesses to us, there should be no surprise if we end up suffering persecution. Allegiance to Christ means that we are not allegiant to money, sex, power and the other gods of this world. Living the truly human life in the power of the Holy Spirit is met with resistance, and that hurts us sometimes. Throughout history, some people have lived radically different lives because of their commitment to what is good and right and true according to the gospel. As a result, they have suffered. But in their suffering, Jesus calls them 'blessed', or, to use another translation, 'happy'. How bizarre!

But it's not that suffering is a blessing in and of itself. That would just be sick! Sometimes, suffering that is borne faithfully within Christ's suffering love can be redemptive, transformative even. Jesus' disciples live in the midst of those who resist God's way of life. It can be tiring; it can seem pointless. But Jesus speaks reality and comfort to his people and says that they are actually blessed, they are known, they are loved and they are enfolded into God's gracious work. In their struggle and need, they are blessed; in their sorrow over the state of the world and their own struggle with sin and temptation, they are blessed.

In other words, it is precisely this posture, as opposed to an over-confident triumphalism, that marks them as Christ's disciples. In their longing for the perfect righteousness of God and their desperation for the fullness of his kingdom, they are blessed. In their crying out, through humility and self-denial for God's lordship alone, they are blessed. They aren't victorious or even blessed in and of themselves. The victory and blessing are in living out the apparent weakness of the cross, which is the powerful key to eternal life. If we don't come to God like this, at the end of ourselves, aware of the brokenness in ourselves and God's world, maybe we aren't as 'blessed' as we think.

5 Lament as repentance

2 Corinthians 7:1–13

The church in Corinth is a kaleidoscope of problems. Paul has his work cut out with them. His previous letter was intense, telling the community off for some pretty awful stuff. Unfortunately, this is way beyond issues about their preferred style of music or who is responsible for the youth work. Paul hears that his earlier correspondence was received with the clout he had intended, and many are really upset with him. However, while he had no intention of upsetting anyone for the sake of it, he is glad that their grief served a purpose. His letter clearly caused them to reflect on their ethical behaviour and the failure to be a communion of Christ. Their grief led to repentance. He calls this 'godly grief', which 'produces a repentance that leads to salvation and brings no regret' (v. 10).

Like the Corinthians, we sometimes lament our wrongdoing when it is highlighted to us. That sorrow can serve as a means of prompting us to address things in our life which require repentance. Sometimes we are confronted with our selfishness, or we realise we have hurt someone. Will we sense any grief in our hearts over this, and be prompted to confess our sin and repent? Will we allow ourselves to be alarmed, to long for reconciliation and healing, and to act upon these Spirit-led promptings?

Alternatively, we may become indifferent, proud and closed off from God and others. We might allow ourselves to feel bad, to believe we are a sinner and tell everyone we are a bad person in a great display of piety and religious self-flagellation. But then, we just dust ourselves off and carry on as though nothing changed. This is what Paul calls 'worldly sorrow' and it leads to death (v. 10). This is the clever (and common) way we evade following Jesus. We put on a good performance, convinced that we are faithful, but then nothing changes.

Does our sorrow lead to repentance and new life? Does our feeling exposed cause reflection on our faithfulness to Jesus and our love for others? Do we actually want to live for Christ or for ourselves? When we are challenged about how our lives damage the world around us, do we just feel bad or will we address it? May God give us the grace and indignation to truly lament our sin for Christ's sake.

6 Lament as prophecy

Revelation 21:1–5

There is a type of 'holy dissatisfaction' that bleeds through believers: a longing for God's kingdom to become physically present in every sense. By having our eyes fixed on Jesus, we don't blissfully set our sights on heaven and float through life without a care in the world. That sounds more (super-)spiritual than Jesus! But nor should we curl up into a ball, hide from the big bad world and hold on to our anxious thoughts until the 'afterlife'. We live in the light of God's eternal life. Our entire existence is to be shaped by the ultimate hope we have in Jesus. This means that we cling to his promise that he is making all things new. The very means and ways we live are shaped by this, not just our goals. God will establish his kingdom on earth fully, as it is in heaven, when Jesus returns.

In Revelation 6:10, there is a moment where the cries of the martyrs are heard, longing for vindication. They are instructed to wait. We too must wait. We are not passive, and nor are we pessimistic or overly optimistic. Christ spurs us to live as citizens of a different kingdom, a different reality, a reality of faith, hope and love. We celebrate all that is good and right and true. Also, we lament the spaces where God's kingdom reign is yet to become fully and physically present.

In this regard, many of us have a lot to learn from our black brothers and sisters, whose Christian heritage involves encountering the suffering Christ in the bowels of slave ships, through floggings and on the lynching tree. Black spiritual music involves a haunting mix of sorrow and joy, lament and praise. These songs sometimes contained secret coded meanings, a covert refusal to let their humanity be robbed. Jesus would one day set them free (before or through death). Their spirituality helped them retain dignity amid such demonic dehumanisation. Together they would steal back hope and joy by processing despair and darkness through their songs and prayers. This watered the ground with their tears, and Christ grew eternal life in the face of death and the devil. These people truly rejoiced in their lament, that there will be a day when there are no more tears.

Guidelines

- At least two-thirds of the Psalms would be identified as laments. There are laments over suffering, sickness, persecution, sin, mental instability, betrayal, old age and many other things. How do you feel about praying these psalms? If you struggle to relate to them, it is possible that your prayers may be too individualistic. How might God use the 'prayer book of the Bible' (as Dietrich Bonhoeffer calls it) to form and reorient your prayer life as a disciple in the world?

- The Lord's Prayer is known by heart for many of us. Interestingly, every part of it has the scope for enfolding lament within its words. Reflecting slowly on each phrase, you may want to allow the words to broaden your imagination for prayer. How does this affect the way you pray and your relationship with God, others and the world?

- In our western world, we are wired to think we shouldn't suffer, almost as though we are entitled to always be well and free from trouble of any kind. This often forms the way we respond (often unconsciously) to those who suffer, seeing them as a problem to be solved, rather than a person to be heard. Someone once said that being heard is so close to being loved, that they often seem like the same thing. How can our response to those who suffer be faithful to Christ?

- Think about the challenges we have faced in recent years in terms of Covid-19. Compare that with the ongoing struggle of racism that many of us are ignorant of because of our skin colour. Also, reflect on the increasingly concerning situation of global warming and climate change. How might lament shape our understanding and effectiveness within God's mission in the world?

- There is a faithful way to lament, and an unfaithful way to lament. Faithful lament is grounded in Christ, but we often let our cultural sensibilities dictate what we think that looks like. How might Jesus be speaking to us about how we pray and live more faithfully, biblically and holistically in terms of lament?

- Many of our churches think lament is important, but we do not do it. Why is this? How might we change some of our theological and ethical understandings so that we could recognise the healing power of learning to lament in Christ, as his body on earth?

FURTHER READING

J. Todd Billings, *Rejoicing in Lament: Wrestling with incurable cancer and life in Christ* (Brazos, 2015).

Kathleen D. Billman, and Daniel L. Migliore, *Rachel's Cry: Prayer of lament and rebirth of hope* (Wipf and Stock, 1999).

James H. Cone, *The Cross and the Lynching Tree* (Orbis, 2011).

Michael Jinkins, *In the House of the Lord: Inhabiting the psalms of lament* (Liturgical, 1998).

Cheryl A. Kirk-Duggan, *Exorcising Evil: A womanist perspective on the spirituals* (Orbis, 1997).

Soong-Chan Rah, *Prophetic Lament: A call for justice in troubled times* (InterVarsity, 2015).

John Swinton, *Raging with Compassion: Pastoral responses to the problem of evil* (SCM, 2018).

Repentance and forgiveness

Henry Wansbrough

The human creature is a jumble of jostling motives and desires. We know perfectly well, or at least the Christian knows perfectly well, where our happiness lies, but all too often we fail to seek that happiness and allow our attention to be diverted into false channels, passing whims and unsatisfying objectives. The story of the fall of Adam and Eve is a pictorial analysis of our repeated failures. But time and again, in the cool of the evening, God comes looking for his beloved creatures as they hide among the trees, sews them garments to hide their shame and enables them to stand – a little unsteadily – in his friendship again. This is the history of Israel as told in the Bible, the history also of each one of us, a continual record of failure, repentance and forgiveness.

In the gospels we see the forgiving love of God made incarnate in Jesus. Again and again we see the loving hand of God manifesting itself in the forgiveness of sinners. There is no condition attached, and somehow the realisation of the outflow of love from Jesus attracts the conversion of those he meets. It is as though the divine love which he lives and shows is so powerful that many men and women he meets cannot withstand it and are drawn into conversion.

Lent is the time for conversion and for seeking God's forgiveness. In order to share in Christ's act of loving obedience to his Father in the Passion, we try to live more Christian lives during Lent. It may well be helpful to focus on some particular acts of generosity and forgiveness to others.

Unless otherwise stated, Bible quotations are taken from the RNJB.

1 Forgiveness in the desert

Exodus 32:4–9

The story of Israel is a story of continual failure of Israel and forgiveness by the Lord. Moses is still up the holy mountain when they desert the Lord and induce Aaron to make them a golden bull to worship, the image of the Canaanite god of the storm. Aaron collects their gold jewellery, melts it down and 'out came this calf!' (32:24). Aaron will not even accept responsibility. He tries to escape the blame by pretending it is no more than a calf, and that it shaped itself spontaneously – 'It is not my fault!' Moses intercedes, and God forgives. But this is only the first scene of countless others. The historian who put together the history of Israel from the settlement in Palestine to the end of the kingdoms shapes it to show a continual process of rebellion against the Lord. The process goes in four stages: rebellion, punishment, repentance and forgiveness-and-rescue.

The Lord is a God of forgiveness and mercy. On this first occasion, God at last reveals the meaning of his name, the name which is so sacred and so intimate that it may be pronounced only once a year by the high priest. It was revealed at the burning bush, but its meaning was never given and every Hebrew name has a meaning. After this first rebellion it is revealed: 'The Lord, the Lord, God of tenderness and compassion, slow to anger and rich in faithful love and constancy, forgiving fault, crime and sin' (34:6). The word translated as 'tenderness' is from the same root as is used for a mother's womb. It is the word for an affection that can never fade, based on an irreplaceable physical bond which can never be broken. Can a mother refuse forgiveness to her child? No more can God!

The same strength of feeling is seen by the prophet Hosea. He married a wife who turned out to be loose-living and adulterous. But he called her back again and again; he could never abandon her. In this he saw an image of the love of God for the people of Israel: 'Therefore I am now going to allure her; I will lead her into the wilderness and speak tenderly to her… There she will respond as in the days of her youth' (Hosea 2:14–15, NIV). Just so is God waiting to forgive.

2 King David's repentance

2 Samuel 11:2—12:4

The story of David's sin is unforgettable, so please read the whole story again if you can, in 2 Samuel 11—12!

David committed a double sin: not only did he sleep with another man's wife, but he tried to hide the adultery (and subsequent pregnancy) by urging her husband to sleep with her. When Uriah steadfastly refused, as his army mates were on campaign and no soldier might have sex while on campaign (little did he know that the royal commander-in-chief had done so!), David arranged for him to be killed in battle. Then others might think the baby was the product of a one-night stand with a young widow, which in the morality of those days was a much less serious offence.

However, when trapped by Nathan's parable into admitting his guilt, David unhesitatingly accepts his terrible punishment and does penance. 'The Lord forgives your sin,' says Nathan, but the Lord cannot pretend that it did not happen. To us it seems strange that the punishment is merely visited upon the sinner's son. The same happens to Ahab when he has had Naboth judicially stoned to get his vineyard (1 Kings 21:29). Most poignant is David's final word, 'I shall go to him, but he cannot come back to me' (12:23).

David was a brilliant leader, for whom men would die willingly, a demanding and headstrong lover, a father who loved but could not control his own family. It is hard to read the story of the death of Absalom without sharing David's grief (2 Samuel 18—19). As a man of blood, he was allowed only to set in motion the building of the temple by buying the plot of land where it was to stand (24:21). Why was this 'man of blood' chosen to play such a part in Israel's history, that the Messiah should be known as 'son of David'? A passionate penitent? Is this the secret of his greatness?

3 The Lord's Prayer

Matthew 6:9–13

The evangelist Matthew gathers together the teachings of Jesus into five great discourses. Of these the first is the sermon on the mount, the basic conditions for entry into the kingdom. This starts with the beatitudes, the attitudes needed to win God's favour. It ends with the warning that the path of the kingdom is a narrow gate, not a wide road, and that our house needs to be built on rock not on sand.

In the very centre of the sermon stands the Lord's Prayer, again no doubt a collection of the important prayers of Jesus, three petitions for the honour of God and three petitions for our comfort and well-being. The only one which is stressed by repetition in another form afterwards is the prayer for forgiveness 'as we have forgiven those who sin against us'. This is a dangerous prayer! Have we always already forgiven those who sin against us? Otherwise perhaps we should not dare to put this comparison as a condition. The forgiveness we ask is the forgiveness we have given – and this comes again in the equivalent passage in Mark 11:25. Luke gives us a shorter version of the Lord's Prayer, but that too contains the same dangerous petition: 'For we ourselves forgive everyone who is in debt to us.'

Another of these five great discourses in Matthew's gospel concerns relationships between the members of the community of the disciples (chapter 18). This lays out a process of reconciliation: (1) confront the problem. If that doesn't work, (2) bring witnesses. If that doesn't work, (3) bring the problem to the assembly. In other words, take every possible step to solve the problem.

Jesus demands forgiveness not merely seven times – the perfect number – but seventy-seven times (and this can even be translated 'seventy times seven'). Then nearly half the discourse is given to the parable of the unforgiving servant (18:21–35): a king wipes out his servant's debt of ten thousand talents, a debt running into billions of dollars, which no private person could ever repay. On his way out, the servant seizes on a fellow-servant, throttles him and throws him into prison for a debt of a hundred denarii, a few weeks' wages of a casual labourer. The outraged onlookers report the matter to the king, who hands the first servant to the torturers.

Can we happily pray 'forgive us our trespasses *as we forgive* those who sin against us'?

4 Jesus reaches out to sinners

Luke 7:36–50

Nobody likes tax-collectors (or parking attendants). In the Palestine of Jesus' time, tax-collectors were automatically outcasts, for they worked to gather taxes for the hated Romans. The right to collect taxes was a business, rented out to a firm, and the collectors will have taken their rake-off. If anyone needed forgiveness, it was tax-collectors! The tax-collector Matthew was happily collecting entry-tax from those who passed from one province to another by crossing the River Jordan when Jesus approached and called him to join his company. It happened again later: the little super-tax-collector Zacchaeus shinned up a tree out of curiosity to catch a glimpse of Jesus, and suddenly found himself entertaining the master to dinner. One can feel his delight at this positive offer of forgiveness when he promises to pay back four times the amount he has profiteered (Luke 19:8).

To show that all people are equal in God's sight, Luke takes care whenever possible to pair women with men (e.g. the annunciations to Zechariah and Mary, Simeon and Anna in the temple, the widow's son and Jairus' daughter both raised to life). So Zacchaeus' joy is matched by the tears of the woman who has a bad name in the city. She weeps silently at Jesus' feet, wiping the tears from his feet with her boldly unbraided hair, out of loving gratitude at his forgiveness. Jesus does not harass her or embarrass her with questioning, but quietly accepts her plea and her homage, only contrasting it with the Pharisee's (a stickler for exact observance) lack of courtesy.

From the other point of view, in the parable of the prodigal son: the wastrel has insulted his father by his implied, 'I don't care whether you are alive or dead. I want my money NOW.' Yet when he appears over the horizon, dad throws his dignity to the winds, runs to meet him and will not even let him finish his pretty little prepared speech of apology before enveloping him in a bear-hug (Luke 15:20). God hardly gives us time to voice our repentance before granting his forgiveness.

5 Jesus forgives sin

As part of his introduction of Jesus, Mark begins his account by giving a *crescendo* of amazement at his actions: this unknown stranger calls disciples and they follow; he teaches with his own authority; he cures the sick; he dares to forgive sin; he controls the storm. The incident of the forgiveness is a typical Markan 'sandwich': he often inserts an incident between two halves of another so that they explain each other (for example, the cleansing of the temple between the two halves of the barren fig-tree in 11:12–26). In this instance, the physical healing proves the spiritual healing. It is almost unbelievable that any human being should claim this solely divine power, as Jesus does, claiming to be 'son of man', a mysterious title referring back to the 'son of man' to whom all power on earth is given in Daniel 7:13. It is obvious that sin is so basic and elemental a failure that it can be forgiven only by God.

Another story typical of Jesus is this strangely wandering story of the woman taken in adultery (John 8:1–11). It occurs in different places in different manuscripts of the gospel and it seems more Lukan than Johannine in both theme and vocabulary. Most of all, it is typical of Jesus' attitude to scripture. They bring the woman to Jesus, asking for a decision on a point of law. Jesus stuns them into silence by going more deeply into scripture than their superficial question: sin is a matter for God alone, and Jesus invokes the loving mercy of God – the basic characteristic of God. He does the same in Matthew 19; the Pharisees ask about grounds for divorce, but Jesus goes behind the question to the narrative of creation in Genesis: God made them man and woman so that they should cling together and form one personality which cannot be divided. The same again about the woman married successively to seven husbands in Mark 12:26; Jesus goes behind their question to the deeper understanding: they don't understand the Fatherhood of God, for God still *is* Father of Abraham, Isaac and Jacob, and always will be.

Similarly, in the case of the woman caught in the act of adultery and the typical male assumption that she, rather than the man, is to blame, the answer of Jesus is, 'Has no one condemned you? Neither do I condemn you.'

6 Jesus on the cross

Luke 23:39-49

If there is any scene of forgiveness, it is the final scene of the earthly life of Jesus. On his way up to Jerusalem, Jesus does not threaten reprisals on the city where he will meet his death. Instead, he weeps over Jerusalem, both early in his journey (Luke 13:34–35) and again as he approaches the city (19:41–44); forgiveness is his dearest wish for Jerusalem. Again, as he leaves the city and mounts to Calvary, the women weep for him, but he tells them to weep for themselves and their children (23:28–30). In Luke, the scene of the crucifixion is itself a scene of repentance and answering forgiveness. He prays for the forgiveness of his executioners as they nail him to the cross, 'for they do not know what they are doing' (v. 34). In answer to the prayer of the good thief who shares his execution, he promises forgiveness and immediate entry into paradise. At the end, all the crowds who have been watching return home beating their breasts in horror and repentance.

You may object: it is a scene of repentance, not forgiveness. But repentance implies the sure confidence of the offer of forgiveness. From the first preaching of John the Baptist onwards, the concept of repentance implies a change of life, a change of system of values. To the merchants and travellers who splash through the ford of the River Jordan on the busy east–west trade-route, he urges that they should put the values of the kingdom first, with the implied promise that they will be forgiven. The wonderful thing about forgiveness is that it forges a new bond between forgiver and forgiven. If I can bring myself to admit – even to myself, but better still to the person I have wronged – that I have offended, the relationship between the two of us is stronger than if I had never offended at all. Ask any mother of a naughty or awkward child! The worse the offence, the harder is the apology. The harder the apology, the greater is the love required. The greater the love required, the greater is the love returned.

Guidelines

In these stories from Old and New Testament we have seen the effects of the *hesed* of God. This Hebrew concept has no equivalent in Greek, and is very inadequately translated into English as 'mercy' – 'Lord, have mercy'. But 'mercy' is too patronising, as though a powerful overlord grudgingly lays off torturing a victim. Really the concept is of the family love which binds a family together so that each member supports every other member through thick and thin and never lets go. That is the divine love to which we open ourselves by turning back to God, creeping under the shelter of God's wings. 'How often have I longed to gather your children together as a bird gathers her brood under her wings,' cries Jesus (Luke 13:34). It reaches its fulfilment in forgiveness. That is not the end of the story, for it is our task to show that same *hesed* to others, just as the Lord has shown it to us.

- Should we forgive and forget, or forgive and remember our forgiveness as a bond of love?
- Does God forgive so that no trace of the fault remains?
- Is there anything which God could not forgive?
- Is there anything that God would not forgive?
- What do I need to change in my life?

FURTHER READING

Mark J. Boda and Gordon T. Smith (eds), *Repentance in Christian Theology* (Liturgical Press, 2006).

C.D.F. Moule, *Forgiveness and Reconciliation: Biblical and theological essays* (SPCK, 1998).

Easter in John's gospel: Jesus risen in humility

Richard Martin

It has always seemed odd to me that we spend 40 days in solemn Lenten devotion building up to the three holiest days in our calendar – Good Friday, Holy Saturday and Easter Day – and then, instead of embarking on a joyful Easter season (40 days to Ascension Day) celebrating the resurrection, many of us promptly take a week off and churches more or less close down.

So it is good that we have the chance this week to reflect on the Easter stories. I have limited my choice to those in John's gospel, firstly because we can begin to see the complete picture his accounts combine to present, but also because I think in each John offers us nuances of his particular view of the resurrected Jesus, one that is perhaps a helpful counterpoint to the triumphal Christ portrayed by the apostle Paul (e.g. Ephesians 1:20–23; Philippians 2:9–11; Colossians 1:18–20).

As I hope we will see, in these two final chapters of his gospel, the apostle John shows us that the risen Jesus is just the same in character as was the earthly Jesus – there is absolute continuity. It is Jesus who is risen – he has not suddenly changed into an imperialist. The beatitudes are lived out in his resurrection appearances just as fully as they were in his earthly ministry.

Unless otherwise stated, Bible quotations are taken from the NASB.

1 The race to the tomb

John 20:1–10

In his autobiography *Long Walk to Freedom*, Nelson Mandela described how on a presidential trip his hotel chambermaid was shocked to find he had made his own bed in the morning. He replied that he had made his own bed in prison for all those years – why would he stop now?

And it is a similar little detail in John's first Easter Day story that fascinates me. We are told that Peter and John visit the tomb following Mary's announcement that the body has gone (v. 2). The beloved disciple (I will assume it is John) gets there first, sees the linen cloths that had wrapped Jesus' corpse lying on the ground inside, but stays outside. Peter then arrives. They are breathless no doubt, after their early morning sprint. Peter goes into the tomb and sees the same cloths. He also notices the head cloth in a separate place, 'rolled up' (or 'folded up', ESV) by itself. John then goes into the tomb too, and John 'saw and he believed'.

What was it, I wonder, that John saw which caused this sudden leap of faith? Could it have been the folded headcloth, which Peter perhaps pointed out to him? John had shared pretty basic accommodation with Jesus for up to three years. He would know his early morning habits. And I'm guessing that John sees that headcloth and says to himself – that's Jesus! Only he tidies up as carefully as that, only Jesus folds up his clothes like that. He must have done this – he must be alive!

Now you could use this story to teach your children the divine example of making your bed each morning. But that I would suggest is not the evangelist's intention! Rather, he is showing us that the humble, servant-hearted Jesus who washed his disciples' feet, who carefully sorted out his bed each morning, is still the same in character now that he is risen.

One of Easter's mysteries is that no Bible account tells us what happened in the tomb before the stone was rolled away. But this story gives a hint – and it's an astonishing one. The first thing the risen Christ did was to straighten up his pillow. No chambermaid required!

2 With Mary in the garden

This is a very moving scene. I would love to hear the intonation an expert actor would use to speak the word 'Mary!' There are many nuances to reflect upon in this story, too many for one day.

The point to which I'd like to bring into focus is that according to John the risen Jesus' first 'word' is a question: 'Woman, why are you weeping?' (v. 15). This is in line with the story of the Emmaus Road in Luke 24, in whose gospel the first words of the resurrected Christ are also a question: 'What are these words that you are exchanging with one another as you walk along?'

The more I think about it, the more remarkable this is! Here is Jesus, risen, having been proven right in his assertion that he would rise again, the agony of the cross vindicated and transcended, full of Easter joy – justified surely in appearing in a blaze of glory and making a grand entrance – justified now more than ever in making a triumphant speech. But no. He asks questions. What are we to make of this?

For many, it implies a mission strategy that prioritises responding to people's expressed needs above delivering a set formula of the gospel. Starting where people are mirrors the incarnational approach of God's mission to the world.

There is a further, though related, point. This gospel with which we are entrusted not only tells of (and to be authentic, models) the humility of Christ at Christmas but also his humility after Easter. Christ, on his day of triumph, asks a woman a question – and waits for the answer.

3 An early Pentecost

The church keeps the feast of Pentecost 50 days after Easter, celebrating the gift of the Holy Spirit. If we only had John's gospel, we would celebrate it on Easter Day! Here is a very different Pentecost to that described in Acts 2: no rushing wind, tongues of fire or speaking in other languages – just a gentle breathing. It is almost as if John wants us to remember the story of Elijah at the mouth of the cave (1 Kings 19:9–14) when God is not in the wind, earthquake or fire, but in the still, small breath.

That alone tells us that, for John, the resurrected Jesus is still the same in character as he was when he took upon himself the way of the cross: gentle, humble, meek.

There is a further piece of evidence. In Matthew 28:18–20 the risen Jesus says to the disciples, 'All authority in heaven and on earth has been given to Me. Go therefore… teaching them to follow all that I commanded you.' John's account of this commissioning moment is so very different. There is nothing about the authority of Jesus. Nothing about people obeying his teaching. Rather, Jesus' authority is implied and is immediately delegated to his disciples. They are the ones who now decide which sins can be forgiven and which can't. Theirs are the commands, therefore, that people will be challenged to observe.

In John's account, on Easter Day, Jesus empowers his disciples. This is not to say that he has abdicated responsibility! Just that his trust in them is complete. In his humility, he will leave the earth and let them take his work forwards, inspired by the gentle-graced breath of the Spirit.

4 Thomas restored

This passage is likely so familiar to us. We read it as being about Thomas' doubt and coming to faith. There are many lessons to be learned from that approach, about him and about the community which managed to hold him in fellowship through that week when their beliefs were so radically at odds.

I invite you today to ponder it from another angle. What is John telling us about the resurrected Jesus?

First, he comes (as he did on Easter Day, v. 21) in peace – not judgement or rebuke for Thomas. Jesus is showing mercy to the one whose convictions prevent him from accepting what others have received. Perhaps there are echoes here of the apostle Paul's conversion (Acts 9) after a similarly personal resurrection appearance. Here the risen Jesus shows that forgiveness and restoration are still at the heart of his nature and work.

Second, we see Jesus responding to a need. Thomas has said, 'Unless I shall see… and put my finger… and put my hand' (v. 25). Jesus says, not, 'Never mind all that,' but, 'Place your finger here, and see My hands… take your hand.' He starts at Thomas' point of need and from there allows him to reach the conclusion, 'My Lord and My God!' (v. 28). There is gentleness and sensitivity about the way Jesus encounters the uniqueness of Thomas.

And third, there is in verse 29 a beatitude – 'Blessed are they who did not see, and yet believed.' Here is Jesus gently letting the disciples know that these resurrection appearances are not going to occur indefinitely. He will not routinely appear to back up their mission. Instead they are to be faithful witnesses to his resurrection in the work he is sending them to do (v. 21).

5 Breakfast on the beach

John 21:1–14

The humility of the risen Christ is shown clearly in this passage.

He is continuing his servant ministry. Not this time washing the disciples' feet (John 13:1–5) but cooking them breakfast (v. 12). Interestingly, when the disciples bring ashore their miraculous catch, they find that Jesus has brought his own fish and bread (v. 9) – so he has gone shopping for them, too!

If there are any intended eucharistic overtones here for the church's life, John's focus is surely on Jesus as the host, the one who in abundant generosity provides the bread of life for his followers, serves the meal and blesses their daily work.

As in the appearance to Mary Magdalene (and on the road to Emmaus), Jesus is incognito. The disciples take time to recognise him. It is almost as if he is playing a game with them, and there is mutual delight when the penny drops.

This is how it is going to be in the post-Easter future.

The risen Jesus will always be content to be present incognito, on beaches (the image of boatloads of refugees springs to mind) and elsewhere, in those who are hungry, thirsty, strangers, naked, ill or prisoners (Matthew 25:31–46), and he will self-effacingly wait for people to realise that if they have been serving them they have been serving him.

6 Peter restored

From verse 20 we gather that this conversation between Jesus and Peter is a private one. Jesus knows that sometimes getting away from the hubbub of the group is important; consider Mark 7:33 when Jesus heals the deaf and dumb man. Only John, who is following them, is aware of the exchange and perhaps overhears it.

Did the other disciples know about Peter's denials? John did, because he facilitated Peter's entrance to high priest's courtyard (John 18:16). But the others? Probably not, unless Peter had told them.

What we have here, then, is a very gentle and private meeting, not a public dressing down, in which Jesus and Peter confront hurt. Peter's denials, unlike Judas' betrayal, did not harm Jesus. But they surely hurt him. And now Peter is 'hurt' (or 'grieved', ESV, v. 17) – certainly because he is asked three times, 'Do you love me?', but also surely because in his spirit he is acutely aware of his threefold rejection of discipleship (John 18:17, 25, 27).

In this mutual acknowledgement of hurt, the restoration of their love and friendship can take place. Jesus tells Peter that their deaths will be similar (v. 18) although Peter's will come in old age. In the meantime, his life's task is to look after the sheep: being a true disciple, following Jesus (vv. 20, 22) in showing what a good shepherd is like (John 10:11) – one 'who lays down his life for the sheep'.

Not only, then, does John present the resurrected Christ as continuing the humble, serving, ultimately self-sacrificing way of life that led him to the cross, but here he also lays down that lifestyle as a model for all who, starting with Peter, are called to care for people in his name.

Guidelines

The reflections I have offered here arise out of a combination of Ignatian reading of scripture, in prayerful imagination placing yourself into the scene being described and the practice of *lectio divina*, reading and rereading, asking God's Spirit to let one aspect emerge for you and turning that into prayer.

It would not be in the least surprising, therefore, if you see something different in each of these passages to the facet I have focused upon. All I ask is that you 'consider the possibility' (as my old university lecturer used to say) that there may be something of value here. After all, this is not a competition for correctness but a shared exploration into mystery. Perhaps, too, you could revisit Ignatian and *lectio divina* practice, and see what new riches are unfolded by the Holy Spirit as you read these familiar resurrection stories once again.

- Reread these Johannine Easter stories in the light of the beatitudes (Matthew 5:1–10). How does Jesus display those kingdom values in his post-resurrection appearances?
- What difference would it make to your understanding of the risen and ascended Christ if John's Easter stories were the only ones we had?

Open my eyes, O Lord, that I may see the wonders of your law.
PSALM 119:18

FURTHER READING

Raymond E. Brown, *The Gospel according to John XIII–XXI* (Yale University Press, 2007).

N.T. Wright, *John for Everyone Part 2* (SPCK, 2002), chapters 11–21.

Williams Temple, *Readings in St John's Gospel* (Macmillian, 1940), second series, chapters XIII–XXI.

Colossians

Johannes J. Knecht

Coming to faith both implies a momentous event as well as the beginning of a lifelong process of growth into the likeness of Christ and a dying to our old self. It is so easy to focus on or emphasise one of these two poles more strongly than the other: either see the moment one comes to faith as all-sufficient and forget about personal growth or simply highlight the need for transformation without the proper place of the inbreaking of Christ's salvific work. Both these forms of overemphasis would result in an unhelpful conception of the Christian life and skip over the need for a proper understanding of reconciliation and for the pursuit of discipleship and growth into Christlikeness.

The letter to the Colossians avoids these temptations and provides a wonderfully compelling image of how the moment of reconciliation and 'coming to life with Christ' ought to inaugurate a life of continuously being shaped according to the image and likeness of Christ. It shows the believer's dependency on the Lord, the characteristics of this new Christ-given life and the encouragement to let the knowledge of Christ and his mystery inform and shape all aspects of life.

Even though there is significant discussion about the Pauline authorship of Colossians, in these notes, I will not address this and will refer to the author as 'Paul'.

Unless otherwise stated, Bible quotations are taken from the NIV.

1 Hope, faith and love

Colossians 1:1–8

The opening remarks to the letter to the Colossians relay greetings from Paul and Timothy. Even though it is unsure Paul actually visited the church in Colossae, following the report of Epaphras who preached the gospel to them in the first place, they nonetheless acknowledge them to be 'God's holy people in Colossae' (v. 2). They recognise the believers in Colossae to be their brothers and sisters, which is again underlined by them calling God 'our Father' (v. 2). Paul and Timothy, especially when observing their possible distance from the founding and history of the church in Colossae, show their ultimate investment in God's kingdom instead of human allegiances or honour.

Faith and love are the direct reasons that have led Timothy and Paul to thank God for the Colossian believers. Both these actions, respectively directed to God and their neighbour, show, for Paul, that they have correctly placed their hope in the things to come, as promised in the gospel they have already received. It is their response to the gospel and its hope that brought the Colossians to cling on to Christ in faith. Furthermore, they let the universal reality of the gospel and the call that flows from it regarding their neighbour inspire them to love, as Christ loved them. Hope has sprung faith and love.

In the same way, Paul and Timothy have seen the power of the gospel transform communities, churches and people, so too they see the same Jesus active in Colossae. In Colossae too, God is clearly at work as the works of the gospel (the fruit) is being perceived. Even though it was hope that led to faith and love, something preceded the presence of hope: God's grace (v. 6). The understanding of God's grace led to hope, which in turn led to faith and love. Through the speaking, hearing, explaining and then understanding of God's gracious gospel, the Colossians bear fruit and God's kingdom grows.

2 The knowledge and wisdom of Christ

Colossians 1:9–14

Paul repeats his comments of verse 3, ensuring the Colossians of how often and continuously he prays to God for them to grow in wisdom and understanding. This wisdom and understanding are given by the Spirit, poured out at Pentecost. However, if we read further in the letter, we see that Paul locates the mystery, the wisdom and the knowledge of God in the person of Christ. He is the one in whom true wisdom, understanding and knowledge are found (compare 2:3–4). So, in emphasising the role of the Spirit at this point, Paul seems to suggest that the role of the Spirit is to reveal the mystery of God, which is Christ, to the believers. It is this revelation of Christ by the Spirit that leads to wisdom and knowledge.

Being filled with that wisdom and knowledge, we ought to be able to live a life worthy of God and pleasing to him. We need to be careful here not to see this as Paul suggesting that living a life worthy and pleasing to God is somehow within our own power, apart from the life-changing power of Christ and the Spirit, for living this life pleasing to God is grounded in the grace God gives in the first place (1:6) and the work of the Spirit revealing the mystery of the gospel. However, when the mystery has been revealed to us, when we have come to know Christ, we can live a life pleasing to him, as it is governed by the Son.

Our faith can then, when properly grounded and founded, bear fruit through faithful works, and we can grow to act in accordance with God's will and be patient and full of endurance to run the race. Joyously, thus, we can celebrate the way in which God has brought us into his own family, the holy people of God. Playing with images of light and darkness, Paul underlines once more what this move into the people of God looks like. While before we were captives in a kingdom of darkness, now, being filled with wisdom and knowledge that flows from the mystery of God having been revealed, we may rest in the light (compare John 1), we may rest in the kingdom of the Son.

Having highlighted the life the believers in Colossae are brought into, the last verse of our section today briefly notes that which characterised the darkness: sin. The move from light to darkness includes both these dimensions.

3 Christ: human and divine

Colossians 1:15–20

The Christ-hymn in Colossians 1:15–20 is one of the most famous descriptions of the person and work of Jesus and probably predates the time in which the letter was actually written. It is absolutely packed with theological truth. Throughout the hymn, there is an interplay of the two crucial affirmations of Christ's existence: his being God and his full human existence.

The affirmation of Christ's divinity is seen in a couple of ways. First, Paul ascribes to Christ the central place in the act of creation: all is made through and for him. Like we see in the prologue to the gospel of John and Proverbs 8, Paul's focus here on Christ's centrality in the act of creation serves to include him into the characteristically divine act of creation and associate him with God's divine wisdom. Everything that exists, the whole of created order – whether visible or invisible, in heaven or on earth – finds its origin in the person of Christ: he is centre of all things created. Second, asserting Christ's divinity more forcefully, Christ is said to be 'before all things' (v. 17) and have God's 'fullness dwell in him' (v. 19). So, clearly, Paul aims to show that Christ is fully divine. However, this is balanced out in the rest of the text with suggestions of his humanity, for Christ is claimed to be the 'firstborn over all creation' (v. 15) and has the capacity to suffer and shed blood (v. 20).

The focus on both Christ's humanity and his divinity serves a twofold aim in these couple of verses: it is the ground for understanding the revelation of God in Christ, and it is what makes God's reconciliation with us possible. To the first point, considering that God is invisible and thus outside the reach of normal human sense-perception, the fact that Christ is both God and human makes it possible for him to visibly reveal the invisible God. Second, it is because in Christ humanity and divinity are ineffably united, that God could 'reconcile to himself all things'.

4 Reconciliation

The last point of the previous section is continued here when Paul elaborates further on the nature of the reconciliation experienced by his addressees. Paul set up a 'once-but-now' image in which the previous state of the Colossians was one of distance and alienation from God. This alienation could have a dual implication here: first, harkening back to verse 12, it could imply the distance between Gentiles and God; second, and this is affirmed explicitly in verse 22, it points at the 'evil behaviour', 'blemish' and 'accusation' that placed the hearers far away from God. Quite likely, Paul is playing with both of these concepts here to describe how they were far away from God before.

Again, like in verse 20, Paul stresses the physicality of Christ's earthly existence: it is in and by Christ's physical body and his earthly death that you are now reconciled with God. In the context of Paul's discussion of reconciliation, the parallel between the mentioning of Christ's blood in verse 20 and his physical body in verse 22 invites the hearers and current readers to see their reconciliation in light of the all-encompassing reconciliation spoken of in verse 20. Our being reconciled with God is simply one of the ways in which we see God's 'reconciling to himself all things' worked out.

After recalling the earlier discourse on hope, faith and love, Paul places himself under the authority of the gospel as its servant. It is easy to forget this proper understanding of how we ought to relate to the gospel. We do not own its message; we are not meant to sell it to other people, nor do we have authority over it. Paul reminds us and encourages us that we are merely there to serve the gospel, to follow God's working through it and to listen to where it leads.

5 Suffering and the mystery of Christ

Colossians 1:24—2:5

Paul has a positive understanding of suffering for Christ. For Paul, suffering is a realistic aspect of being a follower of Christ, as suffering stands at the turning point between the old life and the new, the life inaugurated by the life, death and resurrection of Jesus. Suffering for Christ, but also the associated idea of suffering with Christ, is not self-centred in any sense, but rather stands, in Paul's eyes, in the service of Christ's body, the church. James Dunn even suggests that, for Paul here, there is a particular measure of suffering needed for the world to be brought to its final end, a process started with the suffering of Christ himself, but now continued and completed by his Christian followers. It is this latter point, then, that Paul hints at when suggesting there is still something missing 'in regard to Christ's afflictions' (Dunn, pp. 115–17).

Verses 25–27 tie together the message of the gospel Paul had brought to the Colossians, the mystery spoken of here and the person of Christ. What stands at the centre of the gospel, at the heart of the good news proclaimed by Paul, what God had kept hidden, is none other than Jesus himself, who lives in the Colossians. It is he who is the only hope for the glory that flows from being reconciled to God. Since Christ is the core of the good news, the centre of the gospel, he is the only one proclaimed and he is the ground of all teaching and admonition.

The beginning of chapter 2, then, encourages the audience to find the ground of their understanding and the content of their knowing in Jesus. For it is in him alone that true, Godly wisdom and knowledge is found. When it concerns the truth of the gospel, the Colossians and Laodiceans are spurred on to keep their eyes focused on Jesus and not be tempted to look for or listen to arguments about the gospel and God's reconciliation in Christ that go beyond that revealed wisdom.

6 Discipleship and human understanding

Paul describes the life of the believer as one that should be rooted in Christ, being built up continuously when drawing from him, being strengthened by the life that flows from him. 'Being a Christian', then, is not *solely* a one-time event that determines the rest of one's life. No, being reconciled with God is one thing, but Christian growth requires a continuous relationship with the source of life, Jesus himself, and a holding fast to the faith we were taught.

It is easy to see verse 8 as a fundamental rejection of any form of thinking, philosophy or human tradition. This, however, is not the case. Instead, Paul wants to make sure that our understanding of who God is and the gospel, our knowledge of the mystery of God, which is Christ, is governed and ruled by Christ himself. This verse should not be extrapolated and applied to all philosophy, human tradition and thinking per se. Rather, the cosmic dynamics of God's mystery and his reconciliation of 'all things to himself' should reshape the parameters of that philosophy and human tradition. The foundation of knowledge should be the wisdom of God revealed in Christ.

Because of the presence of the fullness of God in Christ and humanity's participation in the humanity of Christ, every human being can be brought to their fullness. In Christ, perfect humanity is on display and graciously made available to those who participate in him. This participation in Christ is inaugurated by a spiritual 'circumcision', which coincides with a burial with Christ in water and resurrection from the dead. In our being raised with Christ from the dead, being made alive, Paul describes the act of atonement in a twofold manner. On the one hand, he describes it as a legal charge being cancelled by nailing it to the cross. On the other hand, he uses the image of the victorious Christ, standing over power and authorities in a public display of power and might.

Guidelines

- Throughout these beginning sections of the letter to the Colossians, there is an emphasis on the interplay between the wisdom of the world and the wisdom and knowledge that flows from knowing the mystery of Christ. It is easy to see these two in tension with one another or to conflate them. How can we helpfully heed the need to place Christ at the heart of our knowing and understanding without completely avoiding human learning?

- The Christ hymn (1:15–20) is one of the most famous sections of this letter. It beautifully lauds the mystery of Christ and the coming together of humanity and divinity in this one person. How does this reality feature in your own life of faith? Why is it important?

- If we read the wider New Testament, but also Colossians, we get the idea that suffering is a serious and real part of being a follower of Jesus. How does this feature in your own life and how do you relate to it? How can the life of Paul help and support us in carrying the challenge of suffering?

1 Powers and authorities

Colossians 2:16–23

Since God in Christ has dealt with the sin that stood against us and because he has disarmed and triumphed over the 'powers and authorities', food-laws, festivals, or holy days are no longer needed in the same way as before. The idea here is not to disregard or ridicule those who still observe those moments or events. Rather, Paul highlights that, since those events were instituted to foreshadow the fullness of Christ which was to come, when Christ came, the reality those instituted events hinted at has come in the flesh. Foreshadowing is no longer needed. Hence, Paul argues that observing these laws, moments and events no longer holds the same value as it did before and we can, therefore, not be judged for not observing them or for observing them incorrectly. Similarly, people who are 'unspiritual' and live without any connection to Christ as the head of his body should not be listened to when they reject or judge the believer. As the body is made to grow by God, those who are not part of the body have no authority over it.

Dying and being resurrected with Christ, seeing our sin nailed to the cross, truly reorders one's relationship with the world around us. The types of rules and habits that used to guide our existing in the world can no longer hold a similar authority. With the coming and reconciliatory work of Christ for his people, those believing in him are brought into a life where 'the elemental spiritual forces of this world' can no longer be seen as a true means of self-restraint. Paul does seem to hint at the fact that aiming to restrain our 'sensual indulgence' is still important, but the road to it runs through Christ and not extreme asceticism or the adherence to creaturely rules.

2 The old and the new life

In this section, Paul plays with the images of life and death, things above and things below or on earth, the old self and the new self. The main aim is to show how dependent we have become on Christ and thus how we should shun or be weary of the things that characterise our old lives.

Bringing together both the images of baptism and the resurrection of Jesus, Paul places this momentous event at the beginning of one's life with Christ as the anchor of what follows. 'Being raised with Christ' is what separates the two poles of new and old life. Because we have come to life with Christ and are introduced into the new way of living, we should be fixing our eyes on Christ, who is above, ruling with God the Father. Considering the participation in the resurrection life of Christ has drawn us out of darkness and has given us true life, the essence of our existence and the core of our identity lies in him and him alone; where Christ is, where Christ appears, there is our only glory.

The fact that the believer is brought into the new life with Christ does not automatically mean that the temptations and qualifications of the old life will disappear immediately. Paul encourages his readers to 'put to death' and to 'rid yourselves' of these sins and temptations (vv. 5, 8). Clearly, the rejection of the old self is an ongoing work which requires the ultimate focus on the life-giving presence of Christ. It is important to note, though, that even though Paul spurs the believers on to actively reject the old life and put on the new, it is God who renews and shapes our new life 'in the knowledge of its creator'. As Christ is the essence of our existence and defines our being after resurrection, in line with 2:16–23, earthly distinctions like descent, social status or religious background do not hold the same fundamental sway.

3 Characteristics of the new life

As those walking in the new life, Paul aligns the identity of the believers, new and old, with the status of the people of Israel: they are the chosen ones, the holy ones, the dearly beloved ones. This address is also a clear repetition of the opening lines of the letter, where Paul calls them 'God's holy people in Colossae'. Drawing more explicitly from the image of the 'putting on of the new life' introduced earlier in the letter, Paul here encourages the recipients of his letter to 'clothe yourselves' with those things fitting of the people of God: compassion, kindness, humility and gentleness (v. 12). A brief suggestion to the forgiveness of Christ indicates that again, for Paul, the ground of these virtues is the Lord himself. Since the Lord forgave you, you should forgive one another. Quite possibly (but not made explicit) Paul similarly sees the compassion, kindness, humility and gentleness grounded in the life of Christ. It ought to be love that rules supreme, though, as it is the binding principle of all the virtues, 'love, which binds them all together in perfect unity' (v. 14).

As the holy, beloved, chosen people of God, the peace and thankfulness of Christ should be ever present. Paul, over the last 17 verses, has convincingly argued that Christ is the absolute core of the existence of the Christian individual and the Christian community. Christ has given us life; he has introduced us to the new way of living; and he has shown us, through his engagement with us, how to live redemptively with one another. So, whatever we individually or as a community of believers do, be it preach, admonish, sing, praise or anything else, we must remember the centrality of Christ in all that we do and all that we are. He deserves our thanksgiving; his love and gospel should be ever present with and among us; and our eyes should be always fixed on him.

4 The household code

Colossians includes a so-called household code, to which we will now turn. To the modern eye, and in many ways rightfully so, the first verse of this section, which encourages the wives of husbands to submit to their husbands, might raise an eyebrow or two. However, a couple of comments are required to nuance a possible kneejerk reaction one might have: first, within the wider Christian logic of neighbourly, self-giving love, submission is required of all who follow Christ; second, submission to the husband was the normal requirement of a wife of a husband in the ancient world, so Paul is not asking anything that would *increase* the distance or inequality between a husband and a wife; third, Paul arguably *decreases* the inequality, not by subverting the request of submission on the part of the wife – which is what is asked of all of those who follow Christ – but rather by increasing the honour a husband is asked to show his wife. This, indeed, is revolutionary in a world where the relationship between a husband and a wife was fundamentally asymmetrical.

In line with the wider tenor of the letter, Christ, the Lord, the master, is presented as the principle that shapes the interpersonal relationships spoken of here. Paul shifts his focus from merely the relationship between a husband and a wife, a child and a father, or a master and a slave, to the manner in which one can adopt a Christlike posture in those situations. With regards to the slaves Paul addresses, one must remember that the fact that he provides a way to understand their work in a Christlike manner in no way reduces the sinfulness of the practice of owning another human being. Within the given framework of the ancient world, Paul in this chapter aims to reduce the created distance between these members of the household, not because he thinks this is the ultimate 'good' presentation of kingdom living, but because his encouragements would move them in the right direction.

5 Prayer and proclamation

'Devote yourselves to prayer, being watchful and thankful.' What a wonderful start to the final sections of this amazing letter. Paul is in chains; he has lost his freedom and writes to the Colossians from his precarious situation. It is from this place of uncertainty that he encourages the Colossians to pray. For Paul, prayer at this point in time includes watchfulness and thankfulness. Watchful, probably because Paul in this particular moment is experiencing the possible implications of being a follower of Christ, but also watchfulness for the opportunities that might come their way to share about the message of Christ and his mystery (compare 4:5–6). Even when imprisoned for his proclaiming of the mystery of Christ, Paul longs to be ready to preach the good news more.

Interestingly, Paul prays for the quality of his preaching and proclamation, for which he is dependent on the grace of God. In this prayer of Paul, we may all find an encouragement to improve, to think through the *how* of our proclamation. Good and upright doctrine and content is paramount, but, in line with Paul's prayer, let us not forget the quality and clarity of our message. When proclaiming, Paul hopes the Colossians may be ever full of grace. With this, Paul probably does not necessarily mean our understanding of 'being gracious' which can tend to the nonchalant or apathetic. Rather, it seems Paul hopes the grace of Christ may be present in their words, salting and giving strength to what they say. This grace, thus includes all the virtues mentioned above, but is probably hinting more at the presence of the mystery of Christ.

The sending of Tychicus and Onesimus highlights the importance of telling the stories of God in our lives, both the challenging aspects of it (possibly, for Paul, his being imprisoned) but also, doubtlessly, the amazing stories of redemption and faith. Through these stories, relayed to the believers in Colossae via the words of Tychicus and Onesimus, Paul hopes to see them encouraged, for the stories concern the same God, the same holy people and the same Christ.

6 Final words in chains

How easy is it to skip the last sections of these classical letters? However, if one looks past the mere mentioning of names, they often hold some very fascinating insights into the world of author, in this case Paul. First of all, Paul worked together with both those of Jewish and Gentile descent. This is worth mentioning as we see in other places of the New Testament hints that there is a bit of a struggle about the place of the Gentiles among the Jewish Christians. Here, Paul is also not making a distinction regarding the level of engagement or the place of either his Jewish or Gentile co-workers: they all work for the kingdom of God regardless of their backgrounds. Nevertheless, Paul does find some comfort in the fact that some other Jewish believers have come to know Christ – possibly because those with a similarly Jewish background will understand his own history better or because it can be seen as God continuing his story with the Jewish people.

Epaphras is also worth mentioning explicitly, especially because of his apparent love for the Colossians and his dedication to intercession. Considering he is 'one of you and a servant of Christ Jesus' (v. 12), his dedication to the well-being of the Colossians is understandable. Finally, this letter gives a beautiful insight into the early stages of the church: many people were moving around, messages were given from one person to the next, a trusted apostle could vouch for the next, Nympha could have a church gather in her house and letters were probably passed around.

The letter ends with a plea for prayer, for remembrance, and one more encouragement for the grace of Christ to be with the believers. This ending, with many personal greetings and messages, gives the letter a very personal feel, so Paul's last words here are very touching: 'Remember my chains. Grace be with you.'

Guidelines

- Paul both emphasises the reality of the new, inaugurated life in Christ and realises the presence of continuing temptations, struggles and characteristic of the old life. What are ways in which we can, on the one hand, actively reject the old life and all it stands for and, on the other hand, actively put on the new life? How does our own work relate to the work of God in shaping us in this?

- Paul prays that he may proclaim the good news clearly. Do you think this is a valid concern? How can striving for clarity in our proclamation and sharing be seen as a spiritual exercise?

- If we assume that Paul does not encourage conceiving of the relationship between a husband and a wife as unequal and if we assume that Paul does not think slavery is a good thing, how do we relate to passages like the household code in Colossians 3? How can we draw from these texts helpfully and faithfully?

FURTHER READING

James Dunn, *The New International Greek Testament Commentary: The epistles to the Colossians and to Philemon* (Eerdmans, 1996).

Become a Friend of BRF
and give regularly to support our ministry

We help people of all ages to grow in faith

We encourage and support individual Christians and churches as they serve and resource the changing spiritual needs of communities today.

Through **Anna Chaplaincy**
we're enabling churches to provide
spiritual care to older people

Through **Living Faith**
we're nurturing faith and resourcing
life-long discipleship

Through **Messy Church**
we're helping churches to reach out
to families

Through **Parenting for Faith**
we're supporting parents as they raise
their children in the Christian faith

Our ministry is only possible because of the generous support of individuals, churches, trusts and gifts in wills.

As we look to the future and make plans, **regular donations make a huge difference** in ensuring we can both start and finish projects well.

By becoming a Friend of BRF and giving regularly to our ministry you are partnering with us in the gospel and helping change lives.

How your gift makes a difference

£2 a month — Helps us to give away **Living Faith** resources via food banks and chaplaincy services

£10 a month — Helps us to support parents and churches running the **Parenting for Faith** course

£5 a month — Helps us to support **Messy Church** volunteers and grow the wider network

£20 a month — Helps us to develop the reach of **Anna Chaplaincy** and improve spiritual care for older people

How to become a Friend of BRF

Online – set up a Direct Debit donation at **brf.org.uk/donate** or find out how to set up a Standing Order at **brf.org.uk/friends**

By post – complete and return the tear-off form opposite to 'Freepost BRF' (*no other address or stamp is needed*)

If you have any questions, or if you want to change your regular donation or stop giving in the future, do get in touch.

Contact the fundraising team

Email: giving@brf.org.uk
Tel: 01235 462305
Post: Fundraising team, BRF, 15 The Chambers, Vineyard, Abingdon OX14 3FE

Registered with
FUNDRAISING
REGULATOR

Bible Reading Fellowship (BRF) is a charity (233280) and company limited by guarantee (301324), registered in England and Wales

SHARING OUR VISION – MAKING A GIFT

I would like to make a donation to support BRF.
Please use my gift for:

☐ Where it is most needed ☐ Anna Chaplaincy ☐ Living Faith

☐ Messy Church ☐ Parenting for Faith

Title	First name/initials	Surname
Address		
		Postcode
Email		
Telephone		
Signature		Date

Our ministry is only possible because of the generous support of individuals, churches, trusts and gifts in wills.

Please treat as Gift Aid donations all qualifying gifts of money made *giftaid it*

☐ today, ☐ in the past four years, ☐ and in the future.

I am a UK taxpayer and understand that if I pay less Income Tax and/or Capital Gains Tax in the current tax year than the amount of Gift Aid claimed on all my donations, it is my responsibility to pay any difference.

☐ My donation does not qualify for Gift Aid.

Please notify BRF if you want to cancel this Gift Aid declaration, change your name or home address, or no longer pay sufficient tax on your income and/or capital gains.

You can also give online at **brf.org.uk/donate**, which reduces our administration costs, making your donation go further.

Please complete other side of form ➲

SHARING OUR VISION – MAKING A GIFT

Please accept my gift of:

☐ £2 ☐ £5 ☐ £10 ☐ £20 Other £ [   ]

by (*delete as appropriate*):

☐ Cheque/Charity Voucher payable to 'BRF'

☐ MasterCard/Visa/Debit card/Charity card

| Name on card |
| |

Card no. [ ][ ][ ][ ] [ ][ ][ ][ ] [ ][ ][ ][ ] [ ][ ][ ][ ]

Expires end [M][M] [Y][Y]   Security code* [ ][ ][ ]   *Last 3 digits on the reverse of the card

| Signature | Date |

☐ I'd like to find out about giving a regular gift to BRF.

For help or advice regarding making a gift, please contact our fundraising team +44 (0)1865 462305

Your privacy

We will use your personal data to process this transaction. From time to time we may send you information about the work of BRF that we think may be of interest to you. Our privacy policy is available at **brf.org.uk/privacy**. Please contact us if you wish to discuss your mailing preferences.

Registered with

FUNDRAISING
REGULATOR

 Please complete other side of form

Please return this form to 'Freepost BRF'
No other address information or stamp is needed

Bible Reading Fellowship is a charity (233280) and company limited by guarantee (301324), registered in England and Wales

GL0123

Overleaf… Guidelines forthcoming issue | Author profile |
Recommended reading | Order and subscription forms

Guidelines forthcoming issue

God's word is 'better to [us] than thousands of gold and silver pieces' (Psalm 119:72, NRSV). The next issue of *Guidelines* gives treasure upon treasure as our contributors unpack God's word and lead us closer to him.

First, we have the continuation of three series from the previous issue. Andy Angel continues taking us through Matthew 15—28, this time looking mostly at Jesus' various confrontations with religious leaders. This is a challenging set of notes in which we hope you will find much to ponder. Alison Lo continues our series through some oft-neglected minor prophets, following on from Pauline Hoggarth's series, looking at Joel, Obadiah, Micah and Zephaniah. Finally, Stephen Finamore brings us part three of his four-part study of Romans. We have 'unwrapped' Romans and 'run with' Romans; this time we are 'rolling with' Romans as we look at chapters 9—12.

We are excited to start a new five-issue series by Bill Goodman, who will be taking us all the way through the Psalms, one book at a time.

We have some wide-ranging themes in the next issue, too. George Wieland gives us a fascinating tour through intercultural Bible reading. His notes are written out of a research project where people from different cultural and ethnic backgrounds read and discuss the same Bible passage: groups of Māori, Samoan, Ni-Vanuatu, Fijian, Indian and Sri Lankan, Burmese, Chinese, Filipino and other readers. Sally Nash also brings us reflections on her PhD topic of shame and the church, looking at different types of shame and what the church can learn from these. Rosie Button brings us a reflection on refugees, which unfortunately is always a relevant topic.

Finally, we have excellent contributions from Steve Walton and Ashley Hibbard on Ruth and Deuteronomy respectively. And in the New Testament, Michael Parsons brings us detailed notes on 2 Peter, while Rosalee Velloso Ewell unpacks Philippians.

The Bible truly is a treasure chest full of gold and silver, and we hope that these reflections will help you further understand what a gift we have in this treasure.

What the Bible means to me: Richard Martin

 The Bible means that I have both a conversation partner and a source of nourishment on my Christian journey.

Sometimes, maybe when I'm saying Morning or Evening Prayer, I'm afraid I treat the Bible like fast food, just swallow it and go. I'm not really listening.

Other times, I'll make time to chew it over and try to extract the full flavours, to let Christ speak. Just now, for example, I'm reading Philemon and trying to envisage the scene when Onesimus got back to Colossae. At times like this, I find surprising richness emerges.

There is also challenge, rebuke. 'Judge not that ye be not judged' – so hard! If only everyone was like me. But Jesus is reminding me (again!) that it's his plan that they aren't. Not every mouthful of Bible food tastes sweet.

I often have to prepare the meal for others, in a sermon, study group or article. That involves being chef and waiter – attending to the message in the text, as well as to the needs of the diners, to give Christ the chance to speak.

I'll be honest, sometimes I find parts of the Bible indigestible. I struggle with those sections where God's love for all seems to be limited by triumphalism, imperialism, the idea of a 'chosen race', intolerance of difference and eternal rejection. But those passages are there, and I try to hear the word of Christ within them.

Perhaps the most significant moment in my Christian thinking journey was when I realised that 'the word of God is a person, and not a book'.

When relating to a book, you can be an expert. You can translate it, study it, analyse it, learn it off by heart. In a sense, you the reader are in control. You can even skip bits you don't like. A person, on the other hand, always has the capacity to surprise you, challenge you and sometimes annoy you!

It's as if I'm on the road to Emmaus, and Jesus, through the inspiration of the Spirit, and through the wisdom of the church in the form of notes, books and speakers, is there, opening the scriptures for me, amid my dullness of heart and slowness to believe. It's part of his answer to my prayer, give us today our daily bread.

The conversation continues….

Recommended reading

Lent is traditionally a time of repentance, fasting and prayer as we prepare to celebrate our salvation at Easter.

In BRF's Lent book for 2023, *Images of Grace*, through daily readings and reflections from Ash Wednesday to Easter Day, Amy Scott Robinson explores different biblical images of repentance, sin, forgiveness and grace, bringing them together in Holy Week as a lens through which to view Christ's work of reconciliation on the cross.

This extract comes from the first week of reflections, 'Images of sin and repentance'.

Then they said to him, 'What shall we do to you, that the sea may quiet down for us?' For the sea was growing more and more tempestuous. He said to them, 'Pick me up and throw me into the sea; then the sea will quiet down for you; for I know it is because of me that this great storm has come upon you.'

JONAH 1:11-12

Jonah is a story about sin, repentance and the unchanging, predictable nature of God's mercy. It is full of rich metaphors for those things. I should mention from the start that, just because I am calling them metaphors, does not necessarily mean that I'm approaching the whole book as a metaphor or parable. It's presented in the Bible as history; but whichever way we read it, I believe that its images can hold the same meanings.

The story opens with God's direct instruction to Jonah to go and preach to Nineveh, which is a 'great city' full of 'wickedness'. Early listeners to the story would only have needed the name 'Nineveh' to understand that these people were the worst of the worst. They were notorious for their cruelty in war and their merciless treatment of their captors. Speaking out against them would have been terrifying, but as we shall see later, fear was not the reason Jonah gave for his refusal to follow God's instruction.

To avoid the task, Jonah attempted to flee God's presence by getting on a boat heading for Tarshish. God responded with a mighty storm which threatened to break up the ship. Jonah, however, was fast asleep. The sailors cast lots to find out which of them the storm was meant for, and when the lot fell on Jonah, they woke him up and started quizzing him.

Jonah had never been anything but honest with the sailors. Apparently he had already told them that he was fleeing from the presence of God (v. 10) but it was only when he gave them some specifics about *which* God he was trying to avoid that they became anxious. Describing God as 'the one who made the sea and the dry land' (v. 9) didn't leave much wiggle room for the idea that the ship might eventually escape God's territory.

Jonah, however, was remarkably calm, all things considered. Seeing that his actions had endangered the lives of other people, he knew at once that the only way the ship could be saved would be if he wasn't on it. His short speech to the sailors was grounded in logic.

Jonah had not yet reached a point of full repentance in his attitude, but his actions represent the beginning of that journey. By asking to be thrown into the sea, Jonah was physically and forcibly removing himself from the thing that was taking him away from God's plan and God's path. He was removing himself from the others who were at risk of being harmed by his sin as well. Jonah was perfectly self aware: he knew exactly what he had tried to do, and seeing the consequences of it, he was prepared to undo it immediately, even if that meant the sacrifice of his life.

Jonah was absolutely clear and certain about the cause of the storm, and its solution: but he also knew that to be thrown into the sea was to be thrown back into the mercy of God.

Jonah's clear-eyed attitude to his own sin led him to take emergency evasive action which we can learn from when we feel we are heading in the wrong direction. What waves have we already caused with our actions? Who stands at risk of being harmed, or caught up in our choices? What is carrying us away from God's plan, and is it possible, even at great risk, to get clear of it? As we shall see, it's better to be in the sea with God than in a boat without him.

To order a copy of this book, please use the order form on page 151 or visit **brfonline.org.uk**.

Prayer is at the heart of BRF's work, and this special illustrated anniversary collection is a celebration of prayer for BRF's centenary year. It can be used in a range of different settings, from individual devotions to corporate worship. Including sections on prayers of preparation, seasonal prayers, and themed prayers for special times and hard times, it is the perfect daily companion to resource your spiritual journey.

The BRF Book of 100 Prayers
Resourcing your spiritual journey
Martyn Payne
978 1 80039 147 5 £12.99 hardback
brfonline.org.uk

To order

Online: **brfonline.org.uk**
Telephone: +44 (0)1865 319700
Mon–Fri 9.30–17.00

Delivery times within the UK are
normally 15 working days. Prices are
correct at the time of going to press
but may change without prior notice.

Title	Price	Qty	Total
Images of Grace	£9.99		
The BRF Book of 100 Prayers	£12.99		
Followers of the Way	£9.99		

POSTAGE AND PACKING CHARGES			
Order value	UK	Europe	Rest of world
Under £7.00	£2.00	Available on request	Available on request
£7.00–£29.99	£3.00		
£30.00 and over	FREE		

Total value of books	
Donation*	
Postage and packing	
Total for this order	

* Please complete and return the
Gift Aid declaration on page 143.

Please complete in BLOCK CAPITALS

Title .... First name/initials .... Surname ....

Address ....

.... Postcode ....

Acc. No. .... Telephone ....

Email ....

Method of payment

☐ Cheque (made payable to BRF) ☐ MasterCard / Visa

Card no. ☐☐☐☐ ☐☐☐☐ ☐☐☐☐ ☐☐☐☐

Expires end ☐☐ ☐☐ Security code* ☐☐☐ * Last 3 digits on the
reverse of the card

We will use your personal data to process this order. From time to time we may send you information
about the work of BRF. Please contact us if you wish to discuss your mailing preferences **brf.org.uk/privacy**

Registered with
FUNDRAISING
REGULATOR

Please return this form to:

BRF, 15 The Chambers, Vineyard, Abingdon OX14 3FE | **enquiries@brf.org.uk**

For terms and cancellation information, please visit **brfonline.org.uk/terms**.

Bible Reading Fellowship (BRF) is a charity (233280) and company limited by guarantee (301324),
registered in England and Wales

BRF needs you!

If you're one of our regular *Guidelines* readers, you will know all about the benefits and blessings of regular Bible study and the value of serious daily notes to guide, inform and challenge you.

Here are some recent comments from *Guidelines* readers:

'... very thoughtful and spiritually helpful. [These notes] are speaking to the church as it is today, and therefore to Christians like us who live in today's world.'

'You have assembled an amazingly diverse group of people and their contributions are most certainly thoughtful.'

If you have similarly positive things to say about *Guidelines*, would you be willing to share your experience with others? Could you ask for a brief slot during church notices or write a short piece for your church magazine or website? Do you belong to groups, formal or informal, academic or professional, where you could share your experience of using *Guidelines* and encourage others to try them?

It doesn't need to be complicated: just answering these three questions in what you say or write will get your message across:

- How do *Guidelines* Bible study notes help you grow in knowledge and faith?
- Where, when and how do you use them?
- What would you say to people who haven't yet tried them?

We can supply further information if you need it and would love to hear about it if you do give a talk or write an article.

For more information:
- Email **enquiries@brf.org.uk**
- Telephone BRF on +44 (0)1865 319700 Mon–Fri 9.30–17.00
- Write to us at BRF, 15 The Chambers, Vineyard, Abingdon OX14 3FE

Enabling all ages to grow in faith

At BRF, we long for people of all ages to grow in faith and understanding of the Bible. That's what all our work as a charity is about.

- BRF's **Living Faith** ministry looks to see our founder Leslie Mannering's vision – to help people 'get a move on' spiritually – fulfilled in the 21st century. Our wide range of resources promotes Bible reading and prayer, our events bring people together to share this journey, and our Holy Habits initiative helps congregations grow in whole-life discipleship.

- We also want to make it easier for local churches to engage effectively in ministry and mission – by helping them bring new families into a growing relationship with God through **Messy Church** or by supporting churches as they nurture the spiritual life of older people through **Anna Chaplaincy**.

- Our **Parenting for Faith** team coaches parents and others to raise God-connected children and teens, and enables churches to fully support them.

Do you share our vision?

Though a significant proportion of BRF's funding is generated through our charitable activities, we are dependent on the generous support of individuals, churches and charitable trusts.

If you share our vision, would you help us to enable even more people of all ages to grow in faith? Your prayers and financial support are vital for the work that we do. You could:

- Support BRF's ministry with a regular donation;
- Support us with a one-off gift;
- Consider leaving a gift to BRF in your will (see page 154);
- Encourage your church to support BRF as part of your church's giving to home mission – perhaps focusing on a specific ministry or programme;
- Most important of all, support BRF with your prayers.

Donate at **brf.org.uk/donate** or use the form on pages 143–44.

Fruit that lasts

I no longer call you servants, because a servant does not know his master's business. Instead, I have called you friends, for everything that I learned from my Father I have made known to you. You did not choose me, but I chose you and appointed you so that you might go and bear fruit – fruit that will last – and so that whatever you ask in my name the Father will give you.

JOHN 15:15–16 (NIV)

In this verse Jesus is speaking to his disciples in the upper room, giving them a farewell and a sending out, words of comfort and empowerment to get them through the coming days. Here he makes it explicit, those gathered in the room are his friends. Their relationship has transcended that of master and servant through the sharing of knowledge. For a servant simply follows the orders of the master, while a friend with profound understanding can take initiative and carry ideas forward – and ultimately bear lasting fruit.

For over 100 years, BRF has been working to share the knowledge of the gospel with as many people of all ages as possible, whether through our Bible reading notes, like those you are now holding, or the wider work of our ministries – Anna Chaplaincy, Living Faith, Messy Church and Parenting for Faith. It is our goal not only to share the Bible but also to give people the tools for building a deeper understanding of and a closer friendship with God, which will then bear fruit in their own lives and in their communities.

Our work is made possible through kind donations from individuals, charitable trusts and gifts in wills. If you would like to support BRF's work you can become a Friend of BRF by making a monthly gift of £2 a month or more – we thank you for your friendship.

Find out more at **brf.org.uk/donate**.

Judith Moore
Fundraising development officer

Give. Pray. Get involved.
brf.org.uk

Please note our new subscription rates, current until 30 April 2024:

Individual subscriptions
covering 3 issues for under 5 copies, payable in advance
(including postage & packing):

	UK	Europe	Rest of world
Guidelines 1-year subscription	£19.05	£26.55	£30.45
Guidelines 3-year subscription (9 issues)	£54.45	N/A	N/A

Group subscriptions
covering 3 issues for 5 copies or more, sent to one UK address (post free):

Guidelines 1-year subscription	£14.85 per set of 3 issues p.a.

Please note that the annual billing period for group subscriptions runs from 1 May to 30 April.

Overseas group subscription rates
Available on request. Please email **enquiries@brf.org.uk**.

Copies may also be obtained from Christian bookshops:

Guidelines	£4.95 per copy

All our Bible reading notes can be ordered online
by visiting **brfonline.org.uk/subscriptions**

GUIDELINES

Guidelines is also available as
an app for Android, iPhone and iPad
brfonline.org.uk/apps

All our Bible reading notes can be ordered online by visiting
brfonline.org.uk/subscriptions

Title .... First name/initials .... Surname ....

Address ....

.... Postcode ....

Telephone .... Email ....

Please send *Guidelines* beginning with the May 2023 / September 2023 /
January 2024 issue (*delete as appropriate*):

(*please tick box*)

	UK	Europe	Rest of world
Guidelines 1-year subscription	☐ £19.05	☐ £26.55	☐ £30.45
Guidelines 3-year subscription	☐ £54.45	N/A	N/A

Optional donation to support the work of BRF £ ....

Total enclosed £ .... (cheques should be made payable to 'BRF')

Please complete and return the Gift Aid declaration on page 143 to make your
donation even more valuable to us.

Please charge my MasterCard / Visa with £ ....

Card no. ☐☐☐☐ ☐☐☐☐ ☐☐☐☐ ☐☐☐☐

Expires end ☐☐ ☐☐ Security code ☐☐☐ Last 3 digits on the reverse of the card

To set up a Direct Debit, please complete the Direct Debit instruction on page 159.

We will use your personal data to process this order. From time to time we may send you
information about the work of BRF. Please contact us if you wish to discuss your mailing
preferences **brf.org.uk/privacy**

Please return this form with the appropriate payment to:
BRF, 15 The Chambers, Vineyard, Abingdon OX14 3FE
For terms and cancellation information, please visit **brfonline.org.uk/terms**.

Bible Reading Fellowship is a charity (233280) and company limited by guarantee (301324),
registered in England and Wales

GL0123

GUIDELINES GIFT SUBSCRIPTION FORM

☐ I would like to give a gift subscription (please provide both names and addresses):

Title .... First name/initials .... Surname ....

Address ....

.... Postcode ....

Telephone .... Email ....

Gift subscription name ....

Gift subscription address --

.... Postcode ....

Gift message (20 words max. or include your own gift card):

....

....

Please send *Guidelines* beginning with the May 2023 / September 2023 / January 2024 issue *(delete as appropriate)*:

(please tick box)

	UK	Europe	Rest of world
Guidelines 1-year subscription	☐ £19.05	☐ £26.55	☐ £30.45
Guidelines 3-year subscription	☐ £54.45	N/A	N/A

Optional donation to support the work of BRF £ ....

Total enclosed £ .... (cheques should be made payable to 'BRF')

Please complete and return the Gift Aid declaration on page 143 to make your donation even more valuable to us.

Please charge my MasterCard / Visa with £ ....

Card no. ☐☐☐☐ ☐☐☐☐ ☐☐☐☐ ☐☐☐☐

Expires end ☐☐ ☐☐   Security code ☐☐☐   Last 3 digits on the reverse of the card

To set up a Direct Debit, please complete the Direct Debit instruction on page 159.

We will use your personal data to process this order. From time to time we may send you information about the work of BRF. Please contact us if you wish to discuss your mailing preferences **brf.org.uk/privacy**

Please return this form with the appropriate payment to:
BRF, 15 The Chambers, Vineyard, Abingdon OX14 3FE

For terms and cancellation information, please visit **brfonline.org.uk/terms**.

Bible Reading Fellowship is a charity (233280) and company limited by guarantee (301324), registered in England and Wales

DIRECT DEBIT PAYMENT

You can pay for your annual subscription to our Bible reading notes using Direct Debit. You need only give your bank details once, and the payment is made automatically every year until you cancel it. If you would like to pay by Direct Debit, please use the form opposite, entering your BRF account number under 'Reference number'.

You are fully covered by the Direct Debit Guarantee:

The Direct Debit Guarantee

- This Guarantee is offered by all banks and building societies that accept instructions to pay Direct Debits.
- If there are any changes to the amount, date or frequency of your Direct Debit, Bible Reading Fellowship will notify you 10 working days in advance of your account being debited or as otherwise agreed. If you request Bible Reading Fellowship to collect a payment, confirmation of the amount and date will be given to you at the time of the request.
- If an error is made in the payment of your Direct Debit, by Bible Reading Fellowship or your bank or building society, you are entitled to a full and immediate refund of the amount paid from your bank or building society.
- If you receive a refund you are not entitled to, you must pay it back when Bible Reading Fellowship asks you to.
- You can cancel a Direct Debit at any time by simply contacting your bank or building society. Written confirmation may be required. Please also notify us.

Instruction to your bank or building society to pay by Direct Debit

DIRECT Debit

Please fill in the whole form using a ballpoint pen and return with order form to:
BRF, 15 The Chambers, Vineyard, Abingdon OX14 3FE

Service User Number: | 5 | 5 | 8 | 2 | 2 | 9 |

Name and full postal address of your bank or building society

To: The Manager	Bank/Building Society
Address	
	Postcode

Name(s) of account holder(s)

Branch sort code

| | | – | | | – | | |

Bank/Building Society account number

| | | | | | | | |

Reference number

| | | | | | | | |

Instruction to your Bank/Building Society

Please pay Bible Reading Fellowship Direct Debits from the account detailed in this instruction, subject to the safeguards assured by the Direct Debit Guarantee. I understand that this instruction may remain with Bible Reading Fellowship and, if so, details will be passed electronically to my bank/building society.

Signature(s)

Banks and Building Societies may not accept Direct Debit instructions for some types of account.

GL0123